DEPRESSION

"PUTTING HUMPTY DUMPTY
TOGETHER AGAIN"

S. D. Burke

authorHOUSE®

AuthorHouse™
1663 Liberty Drive
Bloomington, IN 47403
www.authorhouse.com
Phone: 1 (800) 839-8640t

Published by AuthorHouse 06/29/2016

ISBN: 978-1-5246-0681-7 (sc)
ISBN: 978-1-5246-0680-0 (e)

Print information available on the last page.

Flower paintings and photos by Sylvia Burke

Published by 1st Books Library 2511 West Third Street
Suite 1 Bloomington, IN. 47404

Library of Congress Cataloging-in-Publication Data

Burke, Sylvia

Dedication

To my family and friends who allowed
me to share their stories.

To my husband George for being there
for me through the years!

To our six children: Julie, Jeff, Jodie,
Janie, Jon and Jennifer
Thanks for allowing your stories,
For keeping me in computers,
And for your encouragement.

And to our eleven grandchildren:
Matthew, Lindsay, Natalie, Eric,
Madelynne, Aubrey, Hannah, Tori,
Ryan, Collin, and Daniel.

To friends who have encouraged me
along life's path:
Liz, Patty, Phyllis,
Jewell, Rose, Arlene, JoAnne
Marta, Michele, Carol, and Connie.

And to my editors:
Jodie, Janie, Jen, Carol,
And the Fountain Hills Christian Writers
Again, I thank you!

Putting Humpty Dumpty Together Again

(Christian Help for Depression)

Contents

I. In the Beginning

Who Is Humpty?

For I know the plans I have for you
….plans to prosper you and not to harm you
….plans to give you hope and a future."
(Jeremiah 29:11, 12)

If you have lost your hope …. Your mind is full of negative thoughts… you don't know how to live any more … you are depressed and need to begin again.

You are My Humpty

If you have given up your dreams to take care of a parent, a handicapped child, an Alzheimer patient … unending, difficult days loaded with hard work, anxiety…

You are My Humpty

If you live with constant pain, or chronic disease such as Multiple sclerosis, Parkinson's, Chronic Fatigue Syndrome, Crohn's Disease, lupus… and are facing years of coping…

You are My Humpty

If you are fighting the good fight against cancer,… facing the possibility of death.

S. D. Burke

You are My Humpty

If you have lost a child, a loved one, or a spouse to death, drugs, or alcohol... are buried in grief, feeling lonely and sad...

You are My Humpty

If you are struggling with a difficult relationship... a boss or spouse who is controlling authoritative... a mate not in sync with your spiritual journey... few kind words.

You are My Humpty

If you are a young mother who has given up her career to be home with her children... no one to talk to... no paycheck to reward you... no time for yourself.

You are My Humpty

If you are wounded and abused from a divorce

You are My Humpty

I meet many Humpty's. I have been Humpty. In the pages of this book, I pray you will find hope, comfort, and practical tools that will help you get back into life, to climb back on the wall...
And Begin again.

Who is Humpty?

Humpty Dumpty sat on a wall
Humpty Dumpty had a great fall
All the King's horses and all the King's men
Couldn't put Humpty together again.
(Mother Goose rhyme)

Cracked and broken, Humpty's shell no longer protects him from the pressure, decisions, and demands of the real world. Those who know Humpty and witness the fall think Humpty will never be whole again. Like our little eggman, those of us who lose our hope may feel like we are broken and falling apart.

At the age of 36, I collapsed in depression. Forty-three years later, I still remember feeling exhausted, overwhelmed and ill.

I was disappointed in myself for not being able to shift gears after the birth of our fifth child. It has taken many years for me to understand what happened. Basically, I was surprised to find myself pregnant. Five years had elapsed; all the children were in school. I was anticipating new challenges but instead found myself looking forward to a few more years of diapers. (Thank goodness the paper ones had been designed!)

I considered myself a good mother—kind, gentle, patient, a good teacher, but not very administrative. I rarely found time for **"me."**

As a new Christian, I thought I should look on the interests of my family instead of myself. I focused on helping the children and my husband George fulfill their needs and dreams. I put my dreams on the back burner.

There are times in our lives where we are, in a way, captive to our circumstance… I loved my husband and children. I didn't want out of my life; I was just exhausted with no way to rest and restore myself. (This happens to caregivers, too.)

I hadn't learned that you have little to give, if you don't take care of yourself. But… how could a mother of five take time for a luncheon, golf, tennis, or shopping? How could I buy myself a new dress when two children needed tennis shoes and one needed money for camp?

One night after dinner, I walked upstairs, climbed off the merry-go-round of life and sat down in my rocking chair. I cried and rocked for two weeks.

In desperation, my husband George called our obstetrician. We had moved just before the baby was born. I had no friends, church, or family close by, no wise counselor to tell me God loved me.

My obstetrician recommended George take me to a female psychiatrist she knew. I began a series of weekly visits. (Note: I believe there are many caring psychiatrists, psychologists, and counselors who can help us. At present, there are 52,000 National Board Certified Counselors. Unfortunately, the psychiatrist I visited was not one of these people.)

Forty-five years ago, psychotherapy was much different. The accepted method of talk therapy counseled the professional to wait for the patient to talk. When I had worked in a psychiatric hospital as a student nurse, I was told not to lead the conversation but to wait on the patient no matter how long that took.

Today, psychiatrists and counselors know how to gently lead a person in helpful conversational therapy. I, too, was at fault, as I did not want to co-operate with this style of therapy. I wanted a wise professional to help me see options and choices that I couldn't see for myself and I felt no desire to lead the conversational direction.

I entered the doctor's office. "Mrs. Burke, won't you come in and have a seat."

I took the seat in front of the psychiatrist's desk. As I said, my experience with psychiatric nursing was a hindrance. I knew the game. She didn't speak. Neither did I. We sat in silence each waiting for the other to open with a remark. The pressure was on me. I felt sad.

I knew the next routine also, to blame someone-your mother, father, and husband. No one was to blame for my dilemma. I was nutritionally depleted and needed time to rejuvenate. I felt overwhelmed with my life and unable to cope with the responsibility of five children, a new community and social responsibilities without friends, family or a church to support me. There was no Facebook, smart phones, no texting.

The psychiatrist did not know how to befriend or counsel me. She was a professional, but what I really needed was love, understanding, and a friend.

Fifty dollars an hour, I sighed. She looked up; was I going to speak? The minutes flew by. She wrote a prescription and handed it to me.

"I'm afraid our time is up today. Have your husband fill this prescription and I'll see you in a week."

I thanked the doctor but left her office feeling let down. She was not going to be able to help me. The weekly sessions continued for about a month. I took the medication faithfully. The tears stopped but I began to feel like a zombie—one of the walking dead. The world continued on its orbit spinning along but I seemed to be on the outside looking on. I barely made it through the days. Finally, I got my courage up and approached my husband.

"George, I'd like to talk to you about the psychiatrist. I don't want to see her anymore. We are wasting $50 an hour. She says nothing to help me and I don't want to go anymore. The problem is I won't be able to take the medication (lithium? Before antidepressants) without her supervising it." I rushed on; "it is my life, isn't it?"

George seemed puzzled but relieved. I was sure he didn't enjoy the drives to the psychiatrist nor the $50 an hour. He nodded.

"Okay, hon, it's your life."

I didn't know how I would get along without the medication. I knew I needed help so I prayed an unusual prayer.

"Dear Father in heaven, I ask you to be my Great Psychiatrist, to help me get well, to bring me into a sound mind."

My dear husband became the real mother and father, picking up my slack, trying to encourage me, while he carried out the duties of a bank president at the age of thirty-nine.

Gradually, I picked myself up and decided that the only truth I was sure of was that love would not let my family perish with no mother. I made my bottom line, "What would love do?"

We had another child a year and a half later and I felt that God had given these children to us as a wonderful gift. I would try to be a person they could always count on. I would be there when they fell down with band aids for their lives. I would be their cheerleader, believe in them, try to help them know God and develop into people of character and heart. I put "Sylvia" on hold. I was actually uncomfortable when anyone called me by my first name. There was no "Sylvia," only Mrs. Burke. I had other serious personal problems that God would help me as I was ready.

Today, I realize that God, the reader of our hearts, gave me exactly what I was searching for... unconditional love and acceptance through our children, a great gift. These children would get to know me as both mother and friend. Through these children, the real "Sylvia" would grow and blossom. She wasn't lost. She was in process.

Although God used our children to give me a great deal of love, I realize for some their children may be a source of anxiety and depression. If you are depressed because your child is addicted to drugs or alcohol, or is anorexic, or has chosen a difficult lifestyle, your situation would be different from mine. God will have a plan of relief and comfort for you, too.

During the following years, God taught me all the wonderful things that I share with you in this book.

All the King's horses and all the King's men did not know how to put Humpty together again but God is *The King*. He knows how to put Humpty back together again. It is a growing process.

I still get a little cracked and scrambled from time to time. But as I am ready for another step, His Spirit opens the door to a new truth that restores my mind, heart and body,

Psalm 139 tells us:
"Lord, you have searched me
And you know me.
You know when I sit and when I rise;
You perceive my thoughts from afar.
You discern my going out and my
lying down.
You are familiar with all my ways.
Before a word is on my tongue
You know it completely."

God knows me intimately, "For I know the plans I have for you,.… plans to prosper you and not to harm you, plans to give you hope and a future." (Jeremiah 29:11, 12.)

During these years, my identity like many of yours, came from being a wife and mother.

Later, as the children left the nest, I participated in community activities both in my church and as a volunteer nursing coordinator for Hospice. My identity was connected to the work I did. I was director of Christian education, Hospice nursing coordinator, president of the women's society. I needed to understand who I was based on God's creation of me and not my roles in the family or titles of responsibility.

Who Am I Part B

One of the most healing discoveries came through my work in a women's group at church. We were looking for a video teaching series for small groups of women… something fun, light but powerful. The title, "Your Personality Tree" leapt out as if in neon lights. We sent to the publishing company for the series. From the first moment I heard Florence Littauer (Christian teacher and speaker from California) use her life and husband Fred's to explain personality as God's design and creation, I identified with Florence. I was Florence and in many respects… George was Fred.

One favorite story from the video illustrates their personalities quite well.[1] (paraphrase) On their honeymoon, Florence and Fred were relaxing. A beautiful grape arrangement adorned the coffee table in front of them. Absentmindedly, Florence began to pick grapes off the display and eat them. She noticed Fred's face had clouded over. "Is something wrong, Fred?" she asked.

"Do you like grapes?" he asked.

Florence thought the question quite odd as she must like grapes or she wouldn't have been eating them. "Yes, I do," she replied watching Fred.

Fred reached into his pants pocket and pulled out a nail clipper. He grabbed a cluster of grapes and snipped it off, neatly. "There, that's the way to eat grapes." He smiled and handed Florence the grapes. "When you pick off grapes

---

[1]   Florence Littauer, *Your Personality Tree*, Word Publishing, July 1989.

willy-nilly, you leave ugly stubs sticking up ruining the symmetry of the grape sculpture."

Florence knew she was in a lot of trouble. She was not like Fred. Her mind did not work like his. Florence illustrates the Sanguine-choleric personality. Fred is a perfect Melancholy-choleric. Opposites attract. Opposites need each other.

The video series showed two very different individuals who each had desirable personality traits. This was a great blessing and relief to me because I was feeling inadequate.

Like Florence, I tried to emulate my husband's logical, practical, organized way of life—feeling my personality was deficient. I learned how to make "to do" lists and "to go" lists.

His personality seemed better fitted to running a large household with six children. I regarded my playful, imaginative, make-a-best-friend-in-one-meeting personality as inferior and lost myself trying to become a carbon copy of George.

We have our individual way of looking at life. For example, a few years ago, we purchased a cabin in the White Mountains of Arizona. Nestled in the largest stand of tall pine trees in the world (according to locals), our lot appeared to be in its virgin state—centuries of pine needles lay upon the ground.

The aroma of pine scented the air. Needles crunched beneath my feet as I walked around the woods behind the house. I was awed by nature's cycle. The winter snows and summer monsoons helped by gentle winds brought down the pine needles that made a carpet below the trees to hold moisture and suppress much of the random wild growth of the woods.

The sun filtered through the giant pines. In my imagination, I could see Indians gathering pine needles to stuff their mattresses. Pinecones lay randomly decorating the forest floor. A crafter, I mentally made lovely Christmas trees, wreaths, and other decorations. My eyes envisioned a basket of pinecones on the fireplace hearth waiting to release the wonderful pine scent when added to a winter fire.

My husband saw the pine needles in a different way. He was astounded that the pine needles had never been raked. The greatest danger in a forest is the threat of forest fire. A fire would be spread immediately by the pine needles igniting one tree to the next. (Five thousand acres burned to the ground about seven miles south of us in the spring.)

As a new homeowner, he removed pine needles blocking the roof drains, and raked 100 bags of needles. His logical, practical mind immediately saw the danger to the house. His primary goal was to keep our home safe.

In working with the Littauer's personality study, I realized that God designs personality. Each one of us is unique. The personality instrument that follows is based on flowers. (It corresponds to the sanguine, choleric, phlegmatic, and melancholy personality instrument).

- The Sunflower (sanguine stands out in a crowd of flowers shouting "Look at Me."
- The Chrysanthemum (choleric) is sturdy, lasts a long time, but has a sharp odor. (Often, mums have a sharp tongue.)
- The Rose (melancholy)- has a deep fragrance and beauty but needs attention and care.
- The Lily (phlegmatic) radiates peace and gentleness.

Following is a checklist of personality attributes for each type. Check each trait that you feel is part of your personality. Most people will find that they have more check marks in two categories and are a composite of two personality types. Some will find their personality traits to be equally spread among the four basic types. If you find yourself in this category, you may be a Lily as the Lily is able to be whatever anyone needs her to be. A few of you will be strongly one type. Have a little fun, and take this test.

Four Basic Personality Types

Sunflower (sanguine)

___fun-loving

___center of attention

___friendly

___enthusiastic

___motivator

___spontaneous

___comfortable in large groups

___positive

___unsympathetic

___gift of gab

"the star"

Rose (melancholy)

___reserved, shy

___conservative

___sensitive

___deep, person of few words

___creative, artistic,

___musical

___prefers one on one, small groups

___cup is ½ empty

___detail-oriented

___high expectations

"the writer"

Chrysanthemum (choleric)	**Lily (phlegmatic)**
___serious, logical	___gentle, kind, congenial
___competitive	___stubborn
___assertive	___calm, easy going
___organized	___subtle humor
___goal-orient	___peaceful, peacemaker
___list maker	___compromising
___always right	___difficulty making decisions
___strong opinions	___procrastinator
___judging	___good listener, friend
___president	___attracted to strong people
"the producer or director"	___needs respect
	"the chameleon"

I found great help in this personality study because I needed to know there was nothing wrong in my personality. Our son Jeff took a three-day course as part of his management training. The attendees were given a personality profile which showed out of thirty-three, thirty were the same personality type. My son was the only one of his personality type. Like me, he needs to know that God does not make mistakes. He is the "potter." God created all of us and we are His design. Understanding personality also helps me understand and accept others-a sort of 'I'm-okay-you're-okay' idea. Life would be dull if all flowers were yellow mums. Those blessed with organization and logic need creative, detailed persons in their lives to balance the scale. We complement each other.

Sunflower: The Sunflower is the charismatic lady who enters the coffee hour and draws all women like a magnet. No one wants to miss a word she says because of her gift of gab. Excitement surrounds her. She gestures dramatically with her hands. Positive, smiling and colorfully dressed, she is the center of attention.

The Sunflower feels perfectly comfortable in a large group and often ends up with a best friend in one meeting. In the play of life, she is "the star." Popular but not too sympathetic, she is better at talking than listening.

Smiling, happy, and vivacious, the Sunflower begins to get depressed if life gets too hard. She naturally sees the silver lining better at talking than listening.

As the Sunflower gets older, her Achilles heel can be her gift of gab gone overboard. She may lose friendships as people wish to be in a conversation. Unable to understand, the Sunflower will continue to give monologues on her latest trip, her twenty-five years teaching fourth grade, the book she just finished or movie she last saw because she wants to entertain you.

That's her job, you know!

The Rose!

<u>Rose</u>: Perfect, deep, sensitive, the Rose is the opposite of the Sunflower. The Rose is classic in attire, proper, and conservative. She prefers a small intimate dinner for two to six. The Rose forms a thoughtful opinion which you will need to draw out of her as you would draw water from a well. She is a person of a few well-chosen words. She is easily offended and needs someone in her life to think she is wonderful.

The Rose enjoys time alone to think and be creative. Her creativity may show up in crafts, quilts, watercolor-painting, music, or writing. She may have trouble finishing projects, as she gets lost in the details due to her desire for perfection.

The Rose is suspicious of overly positive people thinking them insincere. Her own temperament leans somewhat to the negative but she is very loyal and family-oriented.

As the Rose grows older, two thorns may give her trouble: focusing on the negative i.e. who's in the hospital, who died, and over-sensitivity.

The Chrysanthemum!

The Chrysanthemum: is a no-nonsense, logical, productive person. If you want something done, ask the busy Mum who tackles problems with industry, concentration and organization. A problem-solver, the "mum" is serious, purposeful and goal-oriented. From age seven, she draws up "to do lists." She is a woman of priorities. Any organization that has a Chrysanthemum for president will accomplish much.

On vacation, a Chrysanthemum researches the sites to see and the best restaurants unfolding a plan to get the most out of each day.

The Chrysanthemum may get depressed if she becomes physically ill. Work and purpose are necessary to her happiness. She helps others but finds it difficult to ask for help and does not enjoy being dependent.

If friends, loved ones, and co-workers don't live up her high expectations, she can be critical and judging.

The Chrysanthemum may give orders forgetting to say, "please and thank you." The risk for her personality type is the danger of becoming bossy and controlling.

The mum is always right. Really!

The Lily!

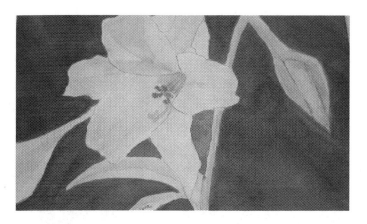

The Lily: The Lily is gentle, kind-hearted, and congenial. A born listener. A good friend. She is a peacemaker with an uncanny ability to find the common ground and soothe ruffled feathers. Unfortunately, she is often a peace-at-all-costs person.

The Lily is cooperative and has trouble saying, "no." She chooses friends who are decisive and dynamic, sometimes giving up personal rights to maintain friendship.

Depression hovers if the important people in her life take advantage of her and do not give her respect.

The Lily is capable of adapting to another's personality making her the chameleon of the group. She is what she needs to be.

If the Lily becomes "more so" in older years, she may become crippled due to her need to be accepted. I hate to say it, but she can even be a little lazy letting the strong mate always drive the car while losing her own long distance driving ability or never paying a bill because her mate is so able.

The Lily is a gentle soul!

Discovering my personality traits helps me realize who God created me to be. I am ME. God knows me. I am His design.

The Holy Spirit living in my heart can balance or compensate for my weaknesses through the addition of the fruits of the Spirit, "love, joy, peace, patience, kindness, goodness, faithfulness, gentleness and self-control." (Galatians 5:22)

God designed many kinds of flowers. He likes variety—a flower garden, not just a bed of roses. When I realize I am God's design, I begin to feel a wonderful peace and acceptance of myself. I don't have to be like anyone. It's all right to be me! How exhilarating... how freeing... how healing!

Humpty must begin somewhere. Discovering who I am is a good place to begin the journey for putting Humpty Dumpty back together again. Though the King's horses and men couldn't put Humpty together again, the *King* can.

Believe it!
Know it!
Live it!

Chapter 1

Who is Humpty?

Exercises:

1. Take the personality quiz? Can you identify the two main types of flowers you are the most like?

2. Think back to when you were a young person. What was your personality like then? Have you changed?

3. Have a personal friend or family member take the quiz for you. Do they come up with the same results you do?

4. What are your personality strengths? Your personality weaknesses?

5. Read 1 Corinthians Ch. 13 and insert your own name. Do you love yourself? Accept yourself?

6. Did Jesus choose only one kind of personality to be an apostle? What personality type do you think these followers were?

Paul	Martha
Thomas	Mary
Peter	John
Barnabas	

7. Look up the fruits of the spirit in (Galatians 5:22). Make a list of these fruits:

   B. How do you see these traits balancing your personality?

8. Does God continue to work on our personality?

Facing My Reality

*"…but speaking the truth in love we are to grow
up in all aspects into Him."* (Ephesians 4:15)

I entered Carol's hospital room. She appeared to be sleeping or else the heavy pain medication was doing its work. I sat down on the only chair in the two-bed room. My eyes caught a verse of scripture taped to the headboard of her bed. It was a verse from Isaiah about eagles. A tape played softly near her bedside, but I couldn't hear the words clearly.

Carol awakened. She weighed 78 pounds. I remembered the first time I saw her. Dwarfed by a big straw sun hat, she was bending over picking strawberries in her patch. She weighed about 150 pounds then. I barely recognized her now. We talked for a few minutes.

As a nurse who had seen death before, I recognized she might be in heaven shortly. Did she know she was dying? She blocked every attempt I made to talk to her in a real way.

I left with the terrible feeling she and her family were in denial about her impending death. If they didn't acknowledge it, she wouldn't die. Later, I learned my suspicions were right. No one was allowed to suggest she might not survive. God would hear her. He had the power to heal.

No one hugged her and said their goodbyes. No one told her they loved her and would see her in heaven. No one prepared her twelve-year-old for losing his mother.

Carol died. God wanted her in heaven with Him. In denying reality, Carol closed all the doors open to her for explaining to her son the natural transition of the soul moving from earth to heaven. As a result, her family was angry and disappointed with God. Despite Carol's faith that God could heal her. He said "No."

Like Carol and her family, I had a difficult time dealing with denial. The Greek actors used masks for their plays. A smiling mask was my costume. It covered fear, anger, fatigue. I was, like Carol, living a lie because I wouldn't deal with the truth.

What was my reality? I was exhausted and tired after our son Jon's birth. I could hardly get through the day and felt unable to attend violin concerts, basketball games, and social business parties. I needed time to regain my strength and let my hormones switch gears. I desperately wanted to sleep through the night but found that impossible while nursing the baby. My laundry seemed unending and I longed for the order that I saw pictured in my home magazines. Yet, I didn't tell anyone how I felt. I just plugged along finding life hard and a lot of work until the day before when I sat down in my rocking chair.

St. Paul tells us to "speak the truth in love" (Eph. 4:15). Pretending everything is fine, when it isn't is actually walking in a lie rather than the truth.

Why was it so hard to say to my family, "I need your help" or to my husband, "I need a rest; there's too much work and not enough fun in my life."

Denying reality can show itself in different ways. I may feel tired or sleep all the time because I spend my energy fighting my current reality. Living in constant anxiety and distress, I may experience a decline in my physical health. (See next chapter, "Depression—Physical Illness?")

Stress stimulates the "fear, fight, flight" chemicals. These chemicals flood our bloodstream until we wear out our immune system.

Take the quiz on the following page. Everyone will check a few of these symptoms, but if you check most of them, you need to acknowledge your reality and begin the search for a new life.

Reality Checklist

1. I have persistent feelings of sadness, hopelessness, "poor little me, no one really knows or cares."

2. I am no longer interested in my job, family, or life.

3. I can't remember the last time I really laughed.

4. I am tired all the time or I am restless and can't sleep.

5. I have little or no interest in sex.

6. I bury myself in work.

7. I use alcohol or drugs to escape, three+ drinks per night.

8. I find exercise too much effort or I have to run three miles a day (do aerobics, etc.) to feel all right.

9. I have no appetite or I eat constantly.

10. I feel like my emotions are out of control, am apathetic, frequently angry or in tears.

11. I never feel really well, frequent headaches, backaches, ulcers or digestive trouble.

12. I avoid people, and conversation. I'd rather be alone.

13. I can't think of one real friend; I have only acquaintances.

14. I have no dreams or goals.

15. I find each day to be one gray sameness.

16. I am glad when the day is over. Life is to be endured; the hum is gone.

17. I have difficulty concentrating, remembering, or making decisions.

18. I worry continually about myself and others.

19. I am compulsively neat, or extremely messy.

20. I think God is far away, does not care, or is punishing me.

21. I have thoughts of death or suicide; I feel hopeless.

We will find help and peace in being an authentic person. Hiding our problems and stuffing our emotions build a dam—a wall that seems to protect Humpty but only prevents others from knowing he is in trouble. An authentic life requires less energy than pretending, but does make us vulnerable. Am I humble enough to admit my needs?

Over 30,000,000 Americans are on antidepressants. I'm convinced for many people depression is the normal transition between and an old life and a new one. Spouses who lose their mate experience this transition. A friend's husband died unexpectedly in his fifties. My friend needed time to grieve and switch from being a happily married woman who shared her life with someone she loved to a single widow who lives alone. It's taking time to face this new reality. And yes, she was depressed for a long time!

When my neighbors' eighteen-year-old son fell off a scaffold washing windows, they needed time to adjust to life without him, to understand where God was in the situation—and yes, to be sad, depressed and to grieve. His death was a harsh reality to face. Depression was a normal and necessary part of working through a terrible experience they had no way to change.

Sometimes, we face the reality of our lives using the depression to problem solve, sort out priorities, change responsibilities, and build a new way of life. If our life isn't working, there's no joy, no contentment. Depression's purpose may be to move us into a new way of life… a simpler way of life… a life with different priorities.

If I am in a difficult marriage with few gentle touches or kind words, I face a long-term reality. Andrea married a man from an Asian culture not realizing both he and his family would look down on her for being Caucasian. She found herself in a servant's role because women in this culture were considered inferior to men. Yet, she did not want to escape her marriage. First, she needed to face her reality, one which would unlikely change.

If I am on twenty-four hour call for a husband who has Alzheimer's, can I become depressed making the transition from normal citizen to giver of care who never rests? Of course. How do I face this new reality? Can I use depression to slow me down so that I can see what options and choices for a happy life still remain: friends or family to share the load, a day care to enable me to have a job, or a mini or maxi vacation to refresh myself?

Continuing in denial can result in physical problems as we will see in our next chapter. Knowing who I am and who God created me to be is a first step. Admitting my reality and beginning "to speak the truth in love" is a second step. But be aware, our bodies mirror the state of our mind and heart health.

Chapter 2

Facing My Reality

1. Think of an example of denial in someone you know. What purpose does it fulfill?

2. Talk about facing reality. What is the cost?

3. Do you have any area of denial in your life? What would happen if you faced this area?

4. Name a first step you could take in the direction of walking in the truth.

5. If you are not ready to acknowledge reality, what are you afraid of?

6. Read the story of David's life found in (2 Samuel, Ch. 12 vs. 15-25.) Tell in your words how David faced his reality.

7. Prayer for help:

"Dear God, I don't know why, but I can't seem to face my own reality.

Show me what to do, Lord. Give me strength through your Spirit to be an authentic person. Forgive me for living my life in denial.

Help me Lord, for I am weak and afraid to tackle my reality alone."

Depression-Physical Illness?

"Above all else guard your heart for
it is the wellspring of life."
(Proverbs 4:23)

The ring of the telephone drew me away from my car packing. In the morning, George and I would leave for a month's vacation in Arizona. I picked up the phone.

"Sylvia, I'm glad I caught you. Julie is having trouble. She woke up hemorrhaging. Barry called 911. The ambulance took her to the hospital." Julie's mother-in-law, Jan, paused to hear my reaction.

I inhaled deeply, "Is she all right? Is the baby all right?" I asked softly.

Jan continued to fill in the details. Could we come and help with seventeen-month-old Matthew? We were packed; the car was ready; only the driving route changed. November would be spent in Minnesota, not Arizona.

Our daughter Julie, not quite seven months pregnant, was experiencing trouble with her pregnancy. Her placenta had pulled away from the wall of the uterus causing hemorrhaging (placenta abruption.)

We arrived at the hospital to find our daughter hooked to heart and fetal monitors. She was also receiving painful injections to stop the contractions that threatened both she and the baby's life.

Our grandson, seventeen-month-old Matthew, did not understand why Mommy preferred to live at the hospital instead of with her favorite little boy. Unable to talk, he let us know his upset by biting whoever took care of him-a parade of helpers. He was quiet and refused to go into Julie's room when we took him to see her at night.

Julie spent two weeks on the high-risk obstetric unit. She longed to be home, so reluctantly, the doctor allowed her to leave the hospital. The first couple of days went well. Matthew played with his toys on her bed and brought her picnics. At night she read him stories. Only once a day was she allowed to get out of bed to take a shower.

The home health nurses visited each day taking her vital signs, the baby's, measuring amniotic fluid. Then, the hemorrhages began again.

Julie returned to the high risk care unit. In the afternoon, I was able to go to the hospital to visit (other relatives were watching Matthew). As I stepped off the elevator, the nurse cornered me and said, "I don't know what you can do but Julie is very upset. I think it's affecting her vital signs."

Sending a jet-winged prayer, I quietly entered the room. Frightened, lonely, and depressed, Julie lay connected to IV's, baby monitors, blood pressure and electrocardiograph equipment.

I looked her in the eye and said: "Honey, you know many people are praying for you and the baby."

"I know, Mom."

"We put the baby in God's hands, didn't we?"

"Yes, Mom."

"Then why don't we just trust Him and rest in His care. Do you have some favorite music that relaxes you?"

Julie asked me to play a CD of hymns. The beautiful piano music filled the room and I closed the door to block all other hospital sounds. Gently, I stroked her face, and her back. She closed her eyes and began to relax. Soon her vital signs and the baby's returned to normal and she rested. Does depression affect us physically? You bet.

Four weeks after Julie became bedridden, Lindsay Grace weighed in at 5 lbs. 1/2 ounce. Although she spent a couple of days on oxygen, Lindsay soon came home weighing 4 lbs. 6 ounces. She was the first baby girl in the Carlson family in 100 years.

As my time to return home drew closer, I received a telephone call from my brother Mike in Florida. Dad was in the hospital. He had suffered a heart attack, perhaps several. His doctor ordered a heart catheterization to show what damage the heart had experienced. Could balloon therapy improve the condition of the heart? I waited for the results. No balloon.

According to the cardiac internist, Dad would in all likelihood have a massive heart attack ending in death if he didn't have immediate bypass surgery. Dad was 84 years young.

I discussed the situation with my husband in Michigan. He told me to do whatever I thought best, warning me that my mother would be the challenge. Considering the severity of the operation Pop would be undergoing and the fact that my brother was in the middle of chemotherapy for cancer, I was a little surprised at his assessment. It did prove to be insightful.

My mother Jenny's health had deteriorated for the past few years. She kept both Dad, my brother Mike, and I busy with near death excursions into the hospital with heart and lung problems. With both her caregivers in worse shape than she was, Mom was devastated. Jokingly I said, "Mom, how does it feel to be the healthiest guy around here?"

A grin broke out on her face. "Not funny, McGee," she retorted.

The vigils and long hours of waiting began to take their toll. Mom became weaker and weaker. Mike and I took her to Dad's new heart doctor who ordered her to stay home from the hospital. He told her to visit Dad by phone. Mike and I took turns driving to the heart institute.

Mom became very quiet and withdrawn. She ate less and less even though we tried to keep a light atmosphere. Her weight dropped into the 90's. She began vomiting every time she ate.

The doctor arranged for a gastroenterologist to see her and run some tests. Did Mom have the flu? Had she eaten something and gotten food poisoning? Did she have an ulcer?

She returned to the cardiac internist who took her hands in his and in a very gentle voice said to my mother, "Jenny, I want you to go home and eat for me. If you don't want me to put you in the hospital. You are getting dehydrated, and you've lost ten pounds."

Great, I thought, *now we will have two in the hospital*. Mike was also experiencing difficulty. The stress was causing his cells to drop dangerously low. He couldn't continue his chemotherapy until his cell count climbed higher. He would need to take special shots to jumpstart his system.

I sent a virtual barrage of prayers toward heaven. When we got home, I said, "Now, Mom, we are going to try something different. You tell me what sounds good. (We had been on tea, toast, jello, applesauce, and crackers.) I don't care what it is; I'll get it or prepare it."

"Well, there is one thing that sounds good."

"What is it, Mom?"

"Braunschweiger on crackers."

I tried not to giggle. "Braunschweiger… Okay, I'll bike up to the grocery and get some. We'll have braunschweiger for supper."

Mom ate the braunschweiger. No vomiting. The next day she said, "I think I could eat pizza."

"Pizza? Well, we'll get pizza then."

"I like Pizza Hut pizza with pepperoni."

Sweet lady… were we seeing depression in disguise? Could depression wear the mask of nausea, vomiting, and weakness?

I haven't done any research to back up my claims but if there is such a thing as common sense and reasoning, I'd bet all my savings on the fact that

Depression can cause physical symptoms.

Both Julie and mother each in her own way expressed physical symptoms that undoubtedly were caused by depression. When our hope level drops, our bodies respond.

Do you have physical symptoms that could be a result of depression? Medical doctors alert us that some patients with colon problems, back pain, and headaches may be signaling depression.

Braunschweiger anyone?

Chapter 3

Depression-Physical Illness?

Exercises:

1. List the physical response to depression in:

Julie
Jenny

2. What helped get them back on track?

Julie
Jenny

3. Using the checklist, what physical symptoms could be related to depression?

4. Did you check anything related to physical problems?

5. Give an example of someone or self that you suspect was depressed but had physical symptoms.

6. Find David's symptoms of depression in Psalm 42.

7. What does the verse in Proverbs 13:12 mean?

S. D. Burke

Prayer:

Oh, Lord, I know that when I am worried, anxious and sad it affects my soul, heart, and body. Help me to be aware if my physical health is camouflaging depression that I may surrender it to you.

II. Where are you, God?

Plugging Into God

"to whom God willed to make known... this mystery...
which is Christ in you, the hope of glory."
(Colossians I: 27) NAS

A computer has a world of power. I can email my grandchildren, make greeting cards, look up stock market quotes, plan a vacation, search a university library, or contact the state department.

I can order a crock pot, a plane ticket, or a diamond ring. I can play a game, download a book, or talk to live chat groups about quilting. I can do a myriad of things on a computer but... it must be plugged into the power source.

Sliding the last breakfast dish into the dishwasher, I listened. Was someone knocking on my laundry room door? At 8:00 a.m.? Curious, I opened the door. My neighbor, Ingrid stood before me, pale and windblown.

"Ingrid, come in. Would you like a cup of tea or coffee?"

Ingrid nodded as I showed her to a seat in my kitchen. "Sylvia, something terrible happened yesterday. Jalil and I went to a new gynecologist. After x-rays, he told me, 'You have a large tumor in your breast. I don't even know if it's worth my time to do surgery.' I felt like the doctor hit me in the stomach with a baseball bat. Jalil put his arms around me. He was so angry with the unkind words of the doctor."

Such terrible news. One minute Ingrid was a lovely wife and mother of three beautiful girls and the next she had received the death sentence.

"Can you help me?" she continued. "I need God and I don't know how to get hold of Him."

There are times in our lives that although we know *of* God we need a deeper, closer walk with Him. We need to feel His presence and know He's on our side. We're sure of one thing; we can't do it alone. But how do we get hold of the power of God? How do we plug into the power source?

Dr. Charles Allen in his book, *God's Psychiatry*[2], tells an interesting and meaningful tale of man who visited his office. In this story, Dr. Allen tells the businessman a way to plug into God.

The businessman rose through the ranks of his company to become its president. Yet, Dr. Allen says, "along the way he left something out and one of the things he did not achieve was happiness. He was a nervous, tense, worried and sick man. Finally, one of his physicians suggested he talk with a minister."

Dr. Allen states, "We talked of how his physicians had given him prescriptions and he had taken them. Then I took a sheet of paper and wrote out my prescription for him. I prescribed the Twenty-third psalm, five times a day for seven days."

Dr. Allen insisted the businessman read the psalm each time-no memorization. He must meditate thoughtfully on each line upon arising, after breakfast, lunch, dinner and before retiring letting the meaning of the psalm saturate his being. Dr. Allen assured the man that in a week things would be different for him. And they were.

---

[2] Dr. Charles L. Allen, *God's Psychiatry*, Fleming H. Revell Co. 1953, p.1

The Twenty Third Psalm

The Lord is my shepherd,
I shall not want.
He makes me lie down in
green pastures;
He leads me beside quiet waters.
He restores my soul;
He guides me in the
paths of righteousness
For His name's sake.
Even though I walk
through the valley
of the shadow of death,
I fear no evil;
for Thou art with me;
Thy rod and Thy staff,
they comfort me.
Thou dost prepare a table
before me in the
presence of my enemies;
Thou has anointed my
head with oil;
My cup overflows.
Surely goodness and loving kindness
will follow me
all the days of my life,
And I will dwell in the
house of the Lord
forever. (NAS)

Let us look closely at the 23'rd psalm. There are many shepherds in life but there is only one Good Shepherd.

The Lord is My Shepherd. But is He? Do we assume because we are sheep, He is our shepherd? Does He know my name? A real shepherd knows each of his sheep. He knows their habits and personalities. He knows their names.

For thirty-three years, I believed I was a Christian. I wasn't a Buddhist, Muslim or Hindu. I was an average American. I must be a Christian.

Then I heard a woman speaker at an Easter retreat say, "Look at the mural behind the altar."

As I looked I saw a painting of Jesus with a little lamb at his side. He stood in front of a door, apparently knocking.

The retreat speaker continued, "He stands at the door of your heart and knocks. The doorknob is on the inside. He will not force His way in. You will have to open the door and invite Him in." (Rev. 3:20)

This was a new concept to me. I had heard the stories of Jesus as a child. I knew He was born as a baby in Bethlehem and was coming back on the Judgment Day. But what was Jesus doing today? I felt He was in heaven but He was definitely not in my heart.

I may know all the stories about Jesus, read the Bible cover to cover, teach Sunday school or sing in the choir, but if I haven't invited Jesus into my own life, I have not opened the door of my heart. He is standing outside waiting for me to let Him in. Only after asking Him into my life can I say, the Lord is My Shepherd. Only then will I be plugged into God. Ingrid needed to invite the Shepherd into her life.

How can having the Lord as your shepherd make a difference in your life? The following stories tell instances when the Shepherd was at work in our own family.

A beautiful lake day. Jeff, our oldest son was running late because it was hard to leave a day of boating and water skiing. Finishing his laundry, he packed the old blue "Maverick," gave me a hug, and prepared to head to the General Motors Institute in Flint, MI where he was an electrical engineering student. My mother's eyes noticed his faded, worn t-shirt and jeans with more holes than cloth.

"Jeff, don't you think you should change your clothes before you leave?"

Jeff smiled, "Now, Mom. I always put on my worst stuff so I can save my clean clothes for school."

I knew I would lose this battle. He was over 18. He gave me that Moms-will-be-Moms look, jumped into his old car and took off. "I'll call you when I get there," he yelled back.

About 9 o'clock I went to tuck eight–year-old Jennifer into bed. When she had finished her prayers, she turned to me, "momma, don't you want to say your prayers, too?"

I had been fighting an anxious feeling that seemed to have Jeff at its root. "Sure, honey."

I prayed for all the family, ending with a special prayer that God would put a shield of protection over Jeff and an angel to watch over him.

Ten o'clock arrived, but no phone call from Jeff. My anxiety intensified. At eleven o'clock the phone rang. It was Jeff. His radiator had overheated so he'd pulled off the highway.

Looking up the embankment, he spotted a house. He climbed up the embankment to ask for help. In the dark, he missed seeing a barbed wire fence. The barbed wire ripped his clothes tearing a six-inch gash in his arm. Bleeding and covered with dirt, he presented a fearful sight to the woman who opened the door. Her eyes saw only the blood and the wound and despite the late hour, she cleaned and dressed it. Then she loaned Jeff her telephone. I was on the other end of the line.

"Should I go to a doctor, Mom? I'm not far from the school."

I spoke in my most professional nurse voice. "As soon as you get back, go to the emergency room, Jeff. They'll check to see if you need stitches and give you a tetanus shot. Are you sure you're all right?"

Jeff returned to his car. A policeman was waiting next to it. He led Jeff to one of the few gas stations open late on a Sunday night.

I shall not want. The Shepherd took care of Jeff's needs. He used our prayers to prepare the woman's heart. She wasn't afraid of his terrible appearance but wanted to help him.

The Shepherd also directed the policeman to guide Jeff to a place where he could get help for his ailing vehicle. *The Lord is a Good Shepherd watching over His sheep.*

My daughter, Janie was a junior in college. One lovely fall day, she and a friend were studying on the lawn of the campus. Growing hot, Janie decided to take off her shoes and wade across the little campus creek to an area where a vendor was selling drinks.

Unknowingly, she stepped on a bee hidden in the grass. As she walked, her face broke out in a red, itchy rash; she had difficulty breathing. Reaching the stand, she asked for a cupful of ice to rub on her toe and her face. By the time she returned to her friend, she felt weak and lightheaded.

"Janie, you look awful. What happened?"

"I think I stepped on a bee."

Beth gathered their books urging Janie to walk to a nearby house. On the way, some sorority sisters offered them a ride. "Can you help me get Janie to the hospital?" Beth said anxiously.

In a few minutes, the girls delivered Janie to the emergency room. The doctor and nurse on duty wasted no time calling a Code Blue. Janie's blood pressure dipped to 30 over 15.

Later, she recalled looking down and seeing some medical people working on a young woman who appeared to be her. She felt no pain and wasn't afraid. The doctor gave her IV adrenaline and a shot of antihistamine. Janie came back to consciousness.

The nurse returned to her friends, "Girls, you did a good job. Five more minutes and it would have been too late."

Though I walk through the valley of the shadow of death, I will fear no evil for Thou art with me; Thy rod and Thy staff, they comfort me... The Good Shepherd was with Janie.

- Beth saved her life by taking her immediately to the hospital instead of back to her room to rest.
- The emergency room nurse immediately called a Code Blue. She didn't waste precious time filling out insurance forms—time Janie didn't have.
- Friends arriving in a car at the moment of need were a crucial coincidence. When God is working,

timing and an apparent series of coincidence often do occur.

The Shepherd is with us in the valley of the shadow of death.

The Shepherd guides us. Our daughter Jodie was anticipating writing a screenplay about a missionary. She was unsure how to structure the story and struggled with how to research real missionaries before beginning the script. She received a phone call from a friend who asked her if she was still thinking of writing a story about a missionary. Susannah told her that her grandmother had started a medical facility and tropical hospital in Deschappelles, Haiti. She needed a companion for a month to drive her and help with her mail. Susannah thought it would be good background material for Jodie's screenplay.

Jodie was amazed at the coincidence but was not at all sure she wanted to go to Haiti in the hot summer season. She struggled with the idea of spending a month in Haiti but since she was thinking of writing "Missionary Man," she felt torn. One of her problems was that she didn't know where her passport and birth certificate were. She thanked Susannah and told her she would think about the offer.

After searching for her passport and birth certificate to no avail, she called and asked, "Mom, do you have my passport and birth certificate?"

George told me that we didn't have Jodie's; he had recently gone through the documents and we had only the two younger kids. I called her back, "Jodie, Dad says we don't have it; you do. But I'll look some more before we come out to visit." (We were taking her for a short visit up the coast of California in a few days.)

Before we left, George insisted we take Jodie's boxes of memoirs with us. I wasn't sure this was a good idea as she had a very tiny apartment. But, he insisted. We loaded fourteen boxes into the van and headed for California. Bored with the scenery, I opened the box nearest me and to my amazement, there in the box was the old passport and birth certificate. The Shepherd had worked through George to load the boxes containing the necessary credentials and guided me to open the one box containing the papers. No other boxes were opened prior to the trip. *The Shepherd was guiding us.*

The Shepherd also helps us in our everyday life. As a new Christian, He led me into a six-year-Bible study *to* graze in *green pastures*. He motivated my husband to buy a cottage on a beautiful lake calming our stressful lives with *the still waters*. He lifted me on his shoulder and carried me when my mother died Christmas Eve 1996, even using Mom's death *to restore our souls* and family relationships.

He is a very good Shepherd. Plug into His kind heart, His wise mind, and great power. They will be at your disposal to help you achieve spiritual, mental and physical health. Humpty needs a Good Shepherd.

Begin your journey by taking the medicine of the 23rd psalm five times a day. Think about it; saturate yourself with the meaning of the words. Invite the Shepherd into your life. *Get plugged into the power source.*

My Shepherd is the Good Shepherd. Is He yours?

Chapter 4

Plugging Into God

Exercises:

I.   Read the 23'rd Psalm five times a day for two weeks.

Questions:

1.   Where are you in your relationship with God? Do you have one?

2.   How do you feel towards God? Be honest. Saul was an enemy of the Christians in the New Testament. Read his story in Acts Ch. 7:59 to 8:3 and Ch. 9. Does the Good Shepherd call him by name?

3.   If you haven't, consider praying the prayer of faith:

Dear Lord, I need your help. Please be my Shepherd. Help me in my life. Forgive me for my sins and failures. I accept Jesus as my Lord and savior. Come into my life and walk with me each day. Be my great Psychiatrist!

4.   *Can you remember a time when a whole lot of circumstances and timing amazingly occurred?*

God's Response to Depression

"Can a mother forget the baby at her breast and
have no compassion on the child she has born?
Though she may forget, I will not forget you!"
(Isaiah Ch. 49:15)

Have you ever sensed another person's impatience with you as a depressed person? Are these familiar words—*Why don't you just pick yourself up and get going?* Has a doctor ever brushed your physical symptoms aside and caused you to feel like a hypochondriac and a loser? If these are peoples' responses, what is God's response?

During the years I was in depression, I often felt I was disappointing God. If I was a Christian, why couldn't I get on top of depression? God seemed far away and I imagined He had little time for failures.

Here is a beautiful passage that shows how wrong we are to think in this manner.

"Can a mother forget the baby at her breast and have no compassion on the child she has borne? Though she may forget, I will not forget you. See, I have engraved you on the palms of my hands; your walls are ever before me." (Isaiah Ch. 49, vs. 15)

What a dynamic passage. Nursing five babies, I can tell you that the milk fills your breast even before the baby cries to nurse. Likewise, in these verses God is gently telling us He knows our needs even before we do. He is closer to us than a real nursing mother. Incredible! He doesn't move away from us. We withdraw from Him. We put up the wall.

In researching the Bible for God's response to depression, I noticed many, if not all, major Biblical characters experienced times of despondence and depression. Let's review a few:

In Genesis, Adam is probably the first depressed person. After eating the fruit of the "knowledge of good and evil," he immediately realized that his disobedience would cost him his intimate relationship with God. Adam was no longer innocent and holy. He knew he was naked and sinful. Afraid, he tried to cover up his nakedness and hid from God. He feared he had ruined his life, and he knew there would be consequences. Nothing would ever be the same.

If our depression is linked to mistakes made in our past, we may feel like Adam, desperate and hiding from God. What was God's response to Adam? Did He fling Adam into a dark abyss? No. In His mercy He asked Adam a simple question, *where are you?* Where are you, Adam, in your relationship with Me? Are we going on together or have you chosen a life of evil?

I think it is very possible that when we go into depression, God's first response may be, 'Where are you?' Adam explained what he and Eve had done. He made excuses. He was not ready to admit his mistake and ask God for help and forgiveness.

The consequences began immediately. God removed Adam and Eve from the garden. They lost their close relationship with Him. Cursed, the ground produced weeds as well as fruit. Eve struggled to have children. Life was no longer easy. Consequences. Our wrong choices have consequences.

God's second response was to cover their nakedness. He killed the first innocent animals and used their skins to cover Adam and Eve. Could this foreshadow the fact that God would have to shed innocent blood and provide His own covering for man's sin—His only son, Jesus? God responded with mercy, forgiveness and help.

Some of us made mistakes in our youth. We made choices that proved to be bad ones. They have followed us for years. It is time to take those mistakes and bad choices to God and ask His forgiveness. (See Chapter 11, "Forgiving God, Self and Others.")

Jesus died to pay for all our sins in advance. We need to let Him cover the guilt and aching in our hearts and move on. And as St. Paul says, "forget what lies behind."

It's depressing when we make a mistake that changes our lives forever. But God is the potter. If the vessel becomes cracked in the process, He can make it into another vessel fit for use.

For many depressed people, sin and error may not be the underlying cause. We may be depressed because we are burned out, used up, and exhausted from living a difficult life.

Elijah the prophet is probably the most detailed and classic case of this kind of depression. The prophet for the northern kingdom of Israel, Elijah (1 Kings Ch. 17-19) was the expressed voice of God in a corrupt culture. Ahab, King of Israel married Jezebel a foreign queen who worshipped the Baal gods. Ahab built altars and high places for Baal worship to please his wife despite God's command "you shall have no other gods before me" (Exodus Ch. 20 vs. 3).

On one occasion while Jezebel was away, Elijah proposed a contest. He challenged the priests of Baal to set up altars and place sacrifices on them. The god who was able to burn the sacrifice without the aid of priests, would be the real God. Elijah drenched his altar with water and the challenge began.

After a dramatic confrontation, Elijah and Yahweh, the true God, emerged the winner. A battle followed and 450 prophets of Baal were killed.

Jezebel was furious. She swore she would kill Elijah. Overcome with fear, Elijah ran for his life. Was he the only Israelite who loved the Lord?

Alone, Elijah traveled a day's journey into the desert. He came to a juniper tree, sat down and told God, "It is enough; now, O Lord, take my life." 1 Kings 19:4 (NAS).

Have you ever reached this point? Elijah gave up; he wanted to die. Elijah had committed no sin. He was burned out and used up doing the work of the Lord. Hungry, thirsty, lonely, and exhausted, he collapsed.

What was God's response? Did He say 'Snap out of it, Elijah?" No, scripture tells us God sent an angel to minister to Elijah (19:5-7). The first order was to replenish his strength. The angel gave him hot baked bread and a jar of water. Then Elijah slept. He was exhausted from all the stress. The angel fed him a second time. Elijah then finished his journey. He headed for Mt. Horeb and entered a cave to sleep.

The word of the Lord came to him, *"What are you doing here, Elijah?"* God listened to Elijah's point of view and description of events. He reassured Elijah that he was not

God's only believer. Seven thousand other people had not bent their knees to the Baal gods.

Then God responded in a strange way. He gave Elijah a new task. He told him to go back and anoint two men as kings and his friend Elisha as prophet. Interesting that doing his regular prophet work for the Lord could be therapy.

What was God's remedy for Elijah's depression?

- The ministry of an angel
- Food and rest
- The Word of God came to Elijah, 'What are you doing here?'
- God listened to Elijah
- God reassured Elijah that he was not alone; others believed in the true God.
- God sent Elijah on a new mission.

The story of Elijah contains wonderful guidelines to help us with depression. Elijah went to Mt. Horeb because it was the mountain of God. *He was seeking God.* This was a good move on his part and should be our first step when we are overcome with depression.

Elijah was exhausted from his ordeal with the showdown. What was his reward. Jezebel swore to kill him.

Depression can better us when we become exhausted with our struggles and battles. Sometimes, there are no rewards or appreciation for our hard work. We, like Elijah, feel alone.

Yet, he was not alone. God knew where he was and what he needed. God knew he was tired, hungry, and thirsty so he sent an angel to refresh him and provide rest and nutrition.

When we have burned both ends and the middle, we don't take very good care of our physical bodies. We may be too busy to eat and don't get a proper amount of sleep. Burned out, our thinking becomes distorted. Elijah's did. He presumed he alone loved God. He felt like he couldn't go on and wanted to quit. He asked God to take him home to heaven. Notice, he didn't think of ending his own life but took his request to God asking Him to take Elijah home to heaven.

God wasn't ready for Elijah to go to heaven. It wasn't Elijah's time yet. He still had work to do for God. When we reach the end of our rope, we need to understand that God still has good plans for our lives, too.

Later, when Elijah's work was finished God actually took him to heaven in a chariot. He didn't die. God is God. He decides our times. His plan is always good for us.

Elijah's depression was caused from exhaustion and burnout. Many of the Humpty's I've met have depression because of the difficult lives they live. Some are looking at years of struggle with chronic disease, cancer, taking care of disadvantaged children, or a spouse with Alzheimer's. God understands. He will be there for you with a cup of refreshment, a friend to lift you up and walk with you, a church to support and cherish you.

In all these examples we see a God who cares, listens, helps, forgives, provides mercy and loving kindness, sends angels to strengthen and encourage. In no case do we see a judging, angry, disgusted God who gives up on the one who has lost hope. If you believe God is disappointed with you, you believe a lie. He is compassionate.

Jesus himself exhibited great depression in the garden the night before He was crucified (Luke Ch. 22:42-45). He sweat giant drops of blood envisioning what He was about to go through. Do we become depressed when we look down the road and see the years of struggle that lie before us? What do I see as my life if I am told I have cancer, or a mate with Alzheimer's?

The disciples could have prayed and lifted Jesus burdens but they didn't understand that He was about to die and they were too tired to stay awake. How terrible for Jesus to see what lay before Him. We know He asked the Father to remove the plan, if He could. We also know that was impossible. Jesus had to die and die a terrible death. How did God respond to Jesus' agony of depression? He sent an angel to strengthen Jesus in the spirit. (Luke Ch. 22:42-44)

There are times when we would like to ask God to take away our present circumstances. And He does not. What He does is promise that He will be with us to strengthen us, to give us understanding and comfort. His goal is not to give us a life without trouble. His goal is to help us "know" God and Jesus and to experience the wonderful love that passes all understanding. Through these difficult times, He will turn our hearts into the likeness of His son.

Satan will try to convince us that no one really knows or cares, not even God. It's a lie. God cares about us. His name is Immanuel, God with us. He will walk with us and comfort us through people, sermons, books, tapes, and by lightning up powerful verses of God's word to illuminate our path.

"Be strong and courageous. Do not be terrified; do not be discouraged, for the Lord your God will be with you wherever you go." (Joshua Ch. 3:1)

Chapter 5

God's Response to Depression

1. Examine your idea of God. Do you think of Him as kind and compassionate or do you think He has forgotten or doesn't care about you? Does this study change your mind?

2. Review the life of Joseph (Genesis Ch. 37)

3. Name several life traumas which might have caused Joseph to be depressed.

   1.

   2.

   3.

4. How did God support and aid Joseph?

5. Look up (Romans 8:28). How was this verse fulfilled in Joseph's life?

Fixing Your Focus

"You will keep in perfect peace him whose mind is steadfast because he trusts in you." (Isaiah 23:3)

One of the problems of depression is the fog that rolls in on the beaches of our mind. An idea or thought will be lost in clouds of forgetfulness. We need to learn to hold onto an idea—to focus.

Our son Jon sprawled in front of the TV set. His eyes were fixed on McGyver, the hero who never carried a weapon, but met trouble with scientific strategies. All voices, actions around him blocked out, Jon concentrated on the drama unfolding. He fixed his attention on McGyver not even hearing me call supper. Jon was focused.

The Bible teaches us several lessons on focusing. In Isaiah Ch. 26:3, the prophet tells us that God will keep us in peace if we keep our eyes on Him.

Caught in a storm, waves lashing their boat, the disciples looked out and saw an apparition (a ghost) walking on the water. They were afraid. (Matt. 14:22-23) Jesus called to them, "Fear not, it is I." Peter answered, "If it is You, tell me to come to You." Peter stepped out of the boat and began to walk on the waves. He was fine till logic and reality set in. His gaze (focus) went from Jesus to the waves (his circumstances) and he began to sink.

Where is our focus? If I am taking care of a husband with Alzheimer's or a child with leukemia, I can take hold of Paul's advice, "I can do all things in Christ who strengthens me," (Philippians 4:13) keeping my hope focused on God or

I can lower my eyes to look at my circumstances—long days of care and stress, lack of sleep, anxiety and fear. I, like Peter, will sink and feel like I am drowning if I shift my focus from Jesus to the waves of circumstance.

I need to know that God will give me grace and strength for the time I need them. I need to trust and keep my eyes on Jesus.

Caregivers have other temptations to face. Exhausted, and burned out they may begin to look inward seeing only their own distress and shifting into survival mode. (If I don't look out for me, who will?) Survival mode may be needed for a short period of respite but shouldn't become our permanent focus. Looking inward is less helpful than looking upward or outward.

Helen H. Lemmel translates this idea into a hymn:

"Turn your eyes upon Jesus; look full in his wonderful face, and the things of earth will grow strangely dim in the light of his glory and grace."

<u>*Create a daily focus for your life.*</u> My mother told me once she awakened each day with the thought, "What lovely thing can I do with today?" A friend's prayer was, "Lord, send me one person I can encourage today with my own life." They were choosing the focus for their day.

In my early days of depression, the fog rolled in and I was unable to live and deal with the everyday. I didn't know how to get started with my day and had difficulty completing simple tasks. The thick fog of depression and unhappiness can paralyze us. Our mind may not want to focus on anything. Even getting out of bed may seem like a huge effort. Your get-up-and-go has got-up-and-gone. Begin putting some structure and routine in your life. *Make a simple schedule.*

1. Awake-lie in bed a moment and think of five things for which you are thankful.
2. Get up.
3. Eat breakfast.
4. Shower, dress.
5. Read a psalm or passage from the Bible.
6. Take a walk
7. Choose a task (laundry, vacuuming) and begin
8. Call a friend, a loved one, or neighbor. Reach out.
9. Relax, take your time, but go forth.

Try to pull out of the lethargy that surrounds you and force yourself to live. When I was at this point in my life, I asked myself the question, 'What would love do?' Love became my incentive. Love would... love could.

If you are overwhelmed instead of immobile and underwhelmed, try my husband's suggestion. Make lists. Write down everything you need to do. Prioritize your list. Check off each task as completed. Don't be paralyzed by all there is to do. Take one job at a time. By the end of the day, you will be surprised how much you accomplish. (Plan those quiet times in, too.)

To do lists, to buy lists, reminders by the phone will help get you out of the fog. Be careful to follow through-if you put something on the stove, keep watch, and turn it off. Stay focused on the task at hand.

There is a children's story my grandchildren love entitled, The *Little Engine That Could*[3]. The little engine had a positive mind focus, "I think I can; I think I can; I think I can."

Faith and hope are at low tide in depression. The loss of faith and hope are two problems antidepressants don't tackle. Do you believe God has good plans for your life? God says, "For I know the plans I have for you, plans to prosper you and not to harm you, plans to give you hope and a future." (Jeremiah 29:11) Ask God to give you a vision of His plans for you.

What are your dreams? Cut out pictures of the life you would like to live and paste them into a scrapbook. Do you picture yourself in a business suit working in an office? Do you see yourself as a mother of two children with a house and picket fence? Do you see yourself surrounded by grandchildren, painting a picture? Ask to see God's plan for you. This scrapbook can be an act of faith—a hope builder. It will focus you on who you can be.

If you are low on gas, and faith and hope are like flat tires, fix *your focus on Jesus!*

---

[3]   Watty piper, George & Doris Haywood <u>The Little Engine That Could.</u> Grosset & Dunlop June 1978. Original The Pony Engine by Mabel C. Bragg Platt & Munk Co. 1930.

Chapter 6

Fixing Your Focus

Exercises:

1. Write down the first thing you think of after waking. Challenge yourself to pick a new morning focus. What will your focus be?

2. Study the story of Noah. What was Noah's focus? Was it realistic?

3. Think about your own circumstances. Are you focused on these circumstances or on God?

4. Look up (Isaiah 26:3). Immerse yourself in the verse. What is the promise in this verse?

5. Pray for a vision of God's plan for your life. Cut out pictures or draw pictures of who you want to be… a grandmother surrounded by her grandchildren, a great cook, a grower of roses, a speaker, homeowner, a writer. By cutting out pictures and pasting them in a scrapbook, you take some steps toward a new life.

III. A New Mind & Heart

Becoming a Thought Detective

Thoughts…

Ralph Waldo Emerson:
*"A man is what he thinks
About all day long."*

Marcus Aurelius:
*"A man's life is what his
Thoughts make it."*

Norman Vincent Peale:
*"Change your thoughts
And you change your life."*

Proverbs 23-7
*"For as he thinketh
in his mind, so is he."*

Becoming a Thought Detective

Where do our thoughts originate? Are all thoughts from God? I never questioned my thoughts. At times, I wallowed in them like a pig in mud. But I never challenged them.

What kind of thoughts parade through my mind? I imagine myself interviewed by Sherlock Holmes:

[Sherlock] "Tell me what thoughts are on your mind?"

[Me] "I try to keep them undercover," I whisper.

[Sherlock] "Uncover them Ma'am; I can't help you if you keep things in the dark. Spit it out."

[Me] "Well, you know—Fear, Anger, Feeling-sorry-for-myself, No-one- really-knows-or-cares thoughts."

[Sherlock] "Running rampant, so to speak?"

[Me] "Yes, detective I seem to have no control."

[Sherlock] "Better police those thoughts. Give them a red light when they try to enter."

[Me] "But detective isn't my mind holy?"

[Sherlock] "Who would send you thoughts of fear, anger, and self pity?"

[Me] "Not God, of course," I reason.

[Sherlock] "Of course not, God is known for saying, "Fear not."

[Me] "Then I have been letting…."

[Sherlock] "Letting darkness parade through your mind, I'm afraid."

All my life I had been letting any thought march into my mind. I accepted them all good or bad but while writing on my computer, I noticed something interesting. If I didn't really want to say something, I highlighted the thought and transferred it into the trash container at the edge of my document or I pressed delete. Could I do this with the thoughts in my mind? Could I monitor my own thoughts and mentally throw them in the trash? If so, what kind of thoughts deserved the trash bin?

Frequently, I had: 'feeling-sorry-for-myself' thoughts, 'poor-little-me-no-one-appreciates-or-knows' thoughts and often I created imaginary scenarios filling my mind with 'what if thoughts… Certainly, most of these thoughts earned a place in the trash bin. (In some computers, the trash bin is called a recycle bin.) Perhaps, some thoughts needed a realigning and recycling.

My mind often raced ahead, creating problems that weren't real, only imaginary. A school bus trip easily turned into a four-hour-wrestling match of *"what if's." What if* the bus rolled off the road and turned over? *What if* no one found the bus to help the children? *What if* my sweet little child was hurt or killed? How would I ever get over my grief?

Did I manufacture false scenarios in my relationship with my husband, friends, and family, mixing the real with the imaginary? These imaginary thoughts destroyed my peace and increased my anxiety. Playing the imaginary thought game uses a lot of emotional energy.

In (1st Peter, Ch. I:13), we read, "Therefore *gird* your minds for action: (NAS) be self-controlled." (NIV)

In the case of vain imagination, I was out of control rather than self-controlled. The Bible teaches us to cast down vain imaginations. Don't let my thoughts take off into *what-if-land*. Nip them right in the bud by turning anxiety over the Lord.

"Lord, it's icy and snowy. Give the bus driver special skills and put a shield of protection around the children on the bus. Send angels to guard them." Cast down the vain imaginations through prayer.

In the first part of the scripture, the word *gird* glowed like a neon light. What did *"gird* your mind" mean? A silly picture of my mother and two of her sisters floated into my mind. It was probably in the 40's. Girdles were a big item. My Aunt Iona stood in our living room stuffing her generous layers into a rubber Playtex girdle.

What was the purpose of the girdle?

- To control loose layers of fat
- To strengthen the back
- To help my aunt appear at her best.

Could girding my mind imply *controlling loose thoughts?* Perhaps. At least I could control loose, negative, destructive, hopeless, self-pity thoughts and the thoughts that made things bigger than life.

How can I gird my mind so that it is *strengthened*? Let's see… I can run positive Bible verses through my mind to counterattack negative thoughts. For example:

Thought: "No one knows and no one really cares."

Bible Verses: "Cast all your anxiety on Him because *He cares for you.*" (1 Peter 5:7).

"Have I not commanded you? Be strong and courageous. Do not be terrified; do not be discouraged for *the Lord your God will be with you wherever you go.*"

I copy the verses that speak to fear, anxiety, assurance onto a 2" by 3" card and put them in my purse.

Whenever I feel alone and can't sense God's presence, I begin to read the verses to reassure myself that He is indeed with me and does care.

I stab the lies, and the negative thoughts with God's word—my sword. In this way, I resist darkness and the bad thoughts flee. Like the purpose of the Playtex girdle, *I strengthen my mind with God's Word* (the sword of the Spirit).

The third purpose of my aunt's girdle was to make her *appear at her best*. It's difficult to see yourself as others see you. Think about people whose spirits are low or who are always worried. Do you enjoy being with them? When you are with them, what effect do they have on you?

On one occasion I had dinner with a woman whose life was falling apart. As she told her story to me, I was overwhelmed. She had financial difficulties, needed a job, had no close friends, felt her church was unsupportive and that God had forgotten her. She was angry, hurt and resentful. Yet, I knew she needed someone to listen, someone to unload her burdens on. She plugged into my peaceful, happy spirit and drained it dry. Ten minutes listening to her story left me exhausted.

Am I doing that to family and friends? If so, I am not *appearing at my best*. I need the girdle. I need to control and eliminate hopeless, negative thoughts not allowing them to consume my mind and spill out on others.

St. Paul tells us "…and we take captive every thought to make it obedient to Christ," (2 Corinthians 10:5). *Taking every thought captive.*

I decided to concentrate on what was happening in my mind when depression started to take over. I stopped and asked myself, *what just happened? What am I thinking?* By doing this analysis, I made my first big breakthrough discovering a root cause of my depression. If I couldn't live up to someone's expectations, or if I felt was letting someone down, I began to have thoughts if inadequacy and low self worth. The heavy cloud of depression and sadness settled over me.

I became a detective learning to recognize the pattern and **taking the thoughts captive**. I replaced them with "I can do all things in Christ who strengthens me" (Philippians 4:13).

After going into all the closets and attics of my mind and spring cleaning. I asked myself a new question. What kind of a mind is true, compassionate, caring, merciful, wise, and discerning? The mind of Christ? According to St. Paul, when we become followers of Jesus and ask Him into our heart, we have access to the mind of Christ. I prayed:

"Transform my mind into a sound mind, Oh Lord, a mind full of hope, ideas and good thoughts. You are the only one who can accomplish the transformation. I know it is you wish for me to have a sound mind. Give me the mind of Christ through your Holy Spirit."

In the weeks that followed, I noticed God changing my mind. He gently pointed out that I was too hard on myself. My expectations were too high. I wasn't Wonder Woman. I wasn't God.

My mind began to view situations from others' points-of-view, not just my own. I knew this has to be God's mind at work. My concentration had been on my view and how people treated me.

Instead of seeing only problems, I began to see options. Jesus is good at the-Jesus-option; look at His answer to those who asked Him if they should pay tribute to Caesar. Since He was God, He didn't have to pay tribute to men, but Jesus replied, "Show me a denarius; whose picture is on it?" 'Caesar's, they replied.' "Then give to Caesar what is Caesar's and to God what is God's." (Luke Ch. 20:24,25)

I began to see life with a sense of humor. God replaced my shortsighted view with a more eternal one. In twenty years, would this problem be important?

He called me to simplicity. "therefore do not worry about tomorrow... each day has enough trouble of its own." (Matt. 6:34) I should leave tomorrow to Him. What were the issues for today?

Other changes occurred in my mind: a quiet peace protected me in difficult situations; creative solution enlightened my mind; my "to do" lists became shorter, my priorities clearer.

I hungered for a quiet time of prayer and Bible reading. If I wanted the mind of Christ, I would need to find out what He thought by feeding on His Word.

The mind of Christ made life gentler and more loving. Christ's mind seemed able to give something to each of my children and even caused me to realize dusting wasn't important to my husband but cleaning the top of the refrigerator was. I *needed the mind of Christ.*

Following the advice of the thought detective I began to police my thoughts. Is this a thought Jesus might think? If not, I arrested the bad thought and deposited it in the trash bin. I realized God would never put thoughts of despair, hopelessness, or fear in my mind.

I learned that if I changed the attitude of my heart to gratitude, I would also change the content of my thoughts.

What is the state of your mind? Have you ever considered your thoughts or do you allow any thought to march into your mind and take over? I challenge you to join me in becoming a thought detective!

Chapter 7

Becoming a Thought Detective

Exercises:

1. Stop when depression begins and ask yourself what triggered your bad feelings. Write what happened just before you felt sad. Become a "thought detective." Keep a notebook.

2. Find a few positive powerful verses in the Bible. Write them on three by five cards. Place them in your purse, wallet, or on your desk. When negative thoughts begin, read these verses over and over until the bad feelings pass. Start with these:

    Philippians 4:6,8;

    Romans 8:28;

    Joshua Ch. 3:1-3

3. Can you remember a time when your imagination ran away with itself? Begin to put the brakes on the *what if's*.

Meditation-A Quiet Time

"....whatever is true, whatever is noble, whatever is right, whatever is pure, whatever is lovely, whatever is admirable-if anything is excellent or praiseworthy-think about such things." (Philippians 4:8)

Although I attended church for many years, Bible reading was not part of my religious heritage. Now things were different. At thirty-three, I had invited the Shepherd into my heart and with His arrival I found a hunger to know the word of God. Not owning a Bible, I visited our church library and checked one out. Like a starving person, I began to devour its words.

One day as I was reading Paul's letter to the Philippians, I came across a verse that appeared to be in italics.

"...whatever is true, whatever is honorable, whatever is right, whatever is pure, whatever is lovely, whatever is of good repute if there is any excellence and if anything worthy of praise, let your mind dwell on these."

I noticed the days when I awoke early and read the Bible, I accomplished my work, was more rested, and more loving with my family. This quiet time became my most treasured part of the day.

In the Bible I read how Moses stopped and saw a bush that was burning but wasn't consumed. God was pleased that Moses took time and stopped to notice. Was God pleased that I was stopping to notice Him and read His Word?

God told Moses to "remove his shoes." As I thought about the scripture, God seemed to be telling me to take off my shoes of concern in the world.

In *a quiet time, my first step is to take off my shoes*. I put my worries and cares aside. I can't interact with God when I'm burdened, so I lay these burdens down before Him, one at a time.

Next, *I speak to the Lord heart to heart telling Him I'm sorry for unloving ways and for the mistakes I've made*. I ask Him to give me a new heart.

Then, *I enter His presence through thanksgiving and praise*. The Psalms are rich with words of thanksgiving and Psalm 100 tells us to be thankful unto Him and bless His name. Psalm 103 states, *"Bless the Lord, O my soul and all that is within me, bless His holy name. Bless the Lord O my soul and forget not all His benefits."* I was unaware that I needed to bless God. I follow the psalmist's words and *remember the many times God has helped me or my family*. I thank Him for my country, home, husband, family, friends, food, and especially for Himself.

How do I enter His courts with praise? Inventing things to praise God for felt uncomfortable and phony to me. But praise is comfortable to the Spirit of God who lives in us. In Psalms 144 through 150 the psalmist begins *"Praise ye the Lord."* If praise is foreign to you, begin reading these psalms. Gradually add your own words of praise.

As my heart is lifted in thanksgiving and praise, I *visualize Jesus sitting on a stone bench in a beautiful garden*. I enter the garden *and sit quietly at his feet*. He reaches down and touches my hair. "It will be all right, you'll see," He says. I listen and enjoy being close to Him.

I open my Bible challenging myself to learn from the people who walked with God. What did Moses, Joseph, David, and Paul do right? What can I learn from their mistakes?

I select a gospel, one of Paul's letters, a book of the Old Testament, or I challenge myself to read the Psalms or Proverbs. During this reading time the Holy Spirit speaks to my present life just as He did the day He told me to fill my mind with things that are beautiful.

Occasionally, as I read I become a Biblical character. In my imagination, I am the adulterous woman, the woman at the well, or Nicodemus. I try to understand what these people felt. I pay particular attention to what Jesus said and did for them:

The Adulterous Woman

(I become the adulterous woman in my imagination.) Someone is knocking at my door. I am engaged in business and not expecting any more customers. When I open the door, a small group of men grab me and pull me into the street. I've seen some of them before; in fact, one is a customer of mine.

The sunlight blinds me. "Where are you taking me?" I ask. They do not answer. From the tassels on the bottom of their clothes I know they are holy men. But today they are rough and rude. "Where are you taking me?" I whisper trying to hide the fear in my voice… Could they be planning to stone me?

As I read I am impressed with the kindness Jesus showed to the woman caught in adultery. He is gentle with sinners; He is gentle with me.

Thinking about the verses I read and putting myself into a character are actually forms of Christian meditation. Different from meditation which calls for emptying the mind, this type of Christian meditation fills the mind with God's words or his attributes and calls on the Christian to think about what he has read. (Sometimes I feel like a cow chewing his cud as I chew on new ideas or wrestle with new challenges.)

I often end my quiet time by reading a hymn. Long ago, I purchased an old hymnal and its beautiful words comfort my heart. If I know the melody, I sing it in my mind. Here is a favorite, *His Eye Is On The Sparrow*:

S. D. Burke

His Eye Is On The Sparrow

Why should I feel discouraged,
Why should the shadows come,
Why should my heart be lonely
And long for Heaven and home?

When Jesus is my portion,
My constant Friend is He;
His eye is on the sparrow,
And I know He watches me;
His eye is on the sparrow,
And I know He watches me.

"Let not your heart be troubled,"
His tender word I hear,
And resting on His goodness
I lose my doubts and fears;
Tho' by the path He leadeth,
But one step I may see;
His eye is on the sparrow,
And I know He watches me;
His eye is on the sparrow,
And I know He watches me

Whenever I am tempted,
Whenever clouds arise,
When songs give place to sighing,
When hope within me dies,
I draw the closer to Him
from care He sets me free.
His eye is on the sparrow,
And I know He watches me.

Refrain:
I sing because I'm happy
I sing because I'm free,
For His eye is on the sparrow,
And I know He watches me.

Civilla D. Martin 1869-1948

Let's look at the elements of a quiet time. (There are many ways to form one.)

1. *Take off your shoes.*
    (Lay your worries and cares before God.)

2. *Ask God to forgive the mistakes of yesterday.*
    (Speak to Him heart to heart.)

3. *Accept His love and forgiveness.*
    (He is faithful to forgive us.)

4. *Enter His gates with thanksgiving.*
    (Thank Him for his blessings.)

5. *Enter His courts with praise.*
    (Bless His holy name!)

6. *Sit quietly at Jesus' feet, listening.*
    (Picture yourself in a garden.)

7. *Open God's word*
    (challenge yourself to read a gospel, psalms.)

8. *Read a hymn or listen to music.*

If this quiet time (one hour) seems long to you, begin with ten minutes reading your Bible quietly and letting God speak to your heart.

Humpty needs to cleanse her mind of worry, anxiety, and fear and begin to fill her mind with the powerful word of God. Join me and become a spiritual athlete. Set up a regular quiet time to fill your mind with everything that is good and beautiful. God will bless you!

Chapter 8

Meditation-A Quiet Time

Exercises:

1. Become a spiritual athlete. Choose 15 minutes, 30 minutes, or an hour for a quiet time. Notice how this affects your day.

2. Read Psalm 119, (vs. 11, 98, 105) What does the psalm say that meditating on God's word will do in my life.

3. Read Psalm 145-150. Pick out phrases that show praise.

4. Read Philippians 4:8. Practice filling your mind with beautiful thoughts.

5. Ask yourself what you watch on television. Does it fit the category of Philippians 4:8?

6. Read Psalm 1, 46, 90, 91, 100, 139. When you become upset read these psalms until you are calm.

7. Choose a story in the Bible. Become one of the characters. Imagine how this person felt.

8. After a week, evaluate what this quiet time has meant to you.

Rose Colored Glasses

"Enter His gates with thanksgiving
and his courts with praise…"
(Psalm 100:4)

Each morning I wake up, open my eyes, smile and think "this is the day the Lord has made, let us rejoice and be glad in it." Or not. It will be the same day despite how I feel. Or will it? Choices. *Grumpy or grateful.*

We are talking about the attitude of the heart. The depressed person is often infected with these viruses:

- "I-feel-sorry-for-myself"
- "why-are-all these-bad-things-happening-to-me?"
- "nobody-really-knows-or-cares"

These viruses invade our heart and produce a poor heart attitude.

One fall day, I dragged myself out of bed. After dressing, I cleaned up the kitchen from breakfast, swept the floor, made beds, gathered the dirty clothes and put them in to the wash. Tears rolled down my cheeks. I could feel the heavy, smothering cloud of depression settling over me. I felt sad, but couldn't tell you why. I really didn't know.

Suddenly, the words, "Enter into His gates with thanksgiving and His courts with praise" floated into my mind. *Where did that thought come from, I wondered? Was it a Bible verse I'd read before?* (Psalm 100:4)

I began to think about the verse. Odd to have a verse pop into my mind. As I thought about the meaning of the verse, I began to understand. My heart felt that God was far away. If I draw near to God through thanksgiving and praise, it was no wonder I didn't feel His presence. Thanksgiving was foreign to my thoughts.

Standing by the washing machine, I looked out my laundry room window. A bushy squirrel was busily collecting nuts and running to hide them under the fallen leaves. I smiled. I would be thankful for the bushy squirrel.

I noticed the fall leaves. When we lived in Michigan I loved to take walks in the fall, listening to the crunch of the dry leaves and observing the glorious red, gold, and coral leaves. I could be thankful for the fall leaves.

I remembered seeing our long-legged teen running for her bus with hair streaming wet from the shower this morning. I was thankful for our six children, They brought excitement and fun into our home.

Home—a spacious house set in the woods planned by my husband and I for our family of eight. How lucky I was to have such a wonderful home.

I was fortunate, too, to have such a hardworking husband. I never had a moment's worry about him becoming interested in another woman. When he said "for better or for worse," he put blinders on. He saw no other women. A gentle man, he carried a lot of responsibility for many years. I was thankful for George.

Suddenly, I noticed the sun shining brightly. The dark cloud had lifted. My heart felt lighter. Why?

THANKSGIVING

The Great Psychiatrist had dropped another powerful weapon into my mind. *It is impossible to be depressed and thankful at the same time.* I knew how to change the attitude of my heart through thanksgiving. Could I develop an attitude of gratitude?

Where is my focus? Do I focus on the positive, the hopeful, the lovely? Trained as a nurse, I was taught to go into a patient's room and basically look for trouble. My focus was 'What's wrong here?'

Looking for what's wrong instead of what's right is useful in dealing with sick people in a hospital room, but as a life pattern, it causes you to miss the joy of life.

Equipped with my new theory of thankfulness, I arrived at my ladies' Sunday school class. Asked by the women's leader to substitute for the day, I planned to do an experiment. I told the ladies about my experience with thanksgiving; then I challenged them. "Ladies, let's take a moment and make a list of the irritating qualities we might like to change in our husbands." The pens flew. When all the pens stopped, I told them to turn their paper over.

"Now," I instructed, "write down all the good qualities you see in your husband." The second list took much longer.

In discussion, each of us confessed the first thing that came to mind about our husband was an irritating quality. One woman who wrote a list of twenty good qualities admitted when she thought of her husband, she could only think how aggravating it was when he threw down his dirty clothes. Another complained about her husband's bad driving. Gone from our mind were the fifteen good qualities which far out-numbered the irritating ones.

We made a pact. Whenever we thought of our husbands, we would replace any negative criticism with a quality for which we were thankful. We would attempt to change our attitudes by thanksgiving.

Another example of a situation my husband and I faced that required a choice of attitude happened when we retired.

My husband and I had decided to sell our Michigan home and retire in Arizona. We told a couple of realtors our Michigan home could be shown while we vacationed in Arizona for the winter months. A local businessman made an acceptable offer. The contract was signed. We returned home to pack and to sell the furniture we were unable to use. We were ready for a new adventure.

Our youngest son, Jon was graduating from Tulane University. We took a break from packing and drove to New Orleans for his graduation. On our return, the moving van was scheduled to pick up our belongings.

The day before we left for Arizona, our buyer's home sale fell through. He didn't have the ability to buy our home. Whoa! With no prospective buyers and half our furniture sold, we put our home back on the market. We could be depressed or choose a different option. Scripture tells us to be thankful in all things and for all things. Could we be thankful even for this new trouble?

I took my eyes off our problems and looked around the neighborhood. I thought of my neighbor, Red—a kind man diagnosed with colon cancer. The prior year, Red had surgery, chemo-therapy, and radiation. The doctor thought he had removed all the growths. It was a clean surgery. But after the winter Red came back from Florida weak and tired. He and his wife returned to the doctor who ran several tests.

The cancer tumors had spread throughout his colon and into his stomach. Little could be done.

In comparing our problem with our neighbors, I decided to be thankful and trust God.

I would choose to enjoy the summer in Michigan putting the house sale in the Lord's hands. I had a choice. I chose not to be depressed.

Friends called one fall and asked me to join them for a drive to see the fall color tour in our area. As we drove, Liz said to me, "Here, look through my sunglasses. Have you ever looked at the leaves through rose-colored glasses?"

The sunglasses transferred me to a world glowing in beauty. Rose-colored trees became shocking crimson; pale blue sky—dazzling cobalt. I was amazed.

Do you need a pair of rose-colored glasses? Is your world a gray, colorless, sameness? When you meet a new person are you looking for what is wrong with them? Is your cup ½ full or ½ empty? *The rose colored glasses are thanksgiving.* We need to see the world through the eyes of thanksgiving.

How can I be thankful if I have some devastating problem—a terrible illness, no job, no love in my life? I can be thankful that in all circumstances I have the Lord on my side fully able to strengthen me for each day. The One who said in Isaiah 43:2,3 *"Fear not… when you walk through the waters, I will be with you; and when you pass through the rivers, they will not sweep over you. When you walk through the fire, you will not be burned; the flames will not set you ablaze. For I am the Lord, your God."*

Have you seen my rose-colored glasses?

Chapter 9

Rose-colored Glasses

Exercises:

1. Before getting up, thank God for five things. Turn the day over to Him, then roll out of bed.

2. Make a list of at least twenty things you're thankful for.

3. Think of a difficult personal relationship. List the qualities that upset you about this person. Turn the sheet over, and write down the person's good qualities. Which list is longer? Try substituting a quality you can be thankful for when thinking of this person.

4. Are you looking for what is wrong in life or what is right. Focus on positives rather than negatives.

5. Look up the following verses:

   James 1:2

   Romans 8:28

   Philippians 4:12

IV. Good Connections

Examining Key Relationships

"Each of you should look not only to your own interest,
but also to the interests of others." (Philippians 2:4)

In the fall of 1998 I toured Rothenburg, a walled city of Germany, with our son Jon, a captain in the Army. Inside the walled city were many quaint small businesses. In front of one of these sat an eight-foot stuffed bear wearing a bright red jacket.

This bear welcomed visitors into a store whose sole product was bears of every size and description. I fell in love with a mama bear dressed in dirndl and apron and a papa bear in a plaid shirt and overalls. These two were seated on a wooden horse teeter-totter. I returned home placed them on my kitchen windowsill, carefully balancing the teeter-totter.

Every time I loaded my dishwasher, I noticed papa bear was holding mama hostage her feet high off the ground. Now, I don't want to accuse anyone of making papa dominant, but I only lived with my husband and a golden retriever, Molly. Which one of you was guilty?

This bear sculpture is a perfect illustration of what often happens in a relationship—the teeter-totter gets out of balance; one person in a relationship becomes more powerful and sometimes too powerful.

My problem with depression caused my relationship with my husband George to get out of balance. Realizing I was not response "able," George stepped up to the plate and took control. I lost his trust and my equality.

It takes a long time to build trust but only a short time to break it. How then can we rebalance the teeter-totter?

- Become an authentic person. St. Paul instructs us to walk in the truth and love. Begin to share feelings and concerns using "I" statements. "Children, I need your help with the dishes after dinner." "George, I need a break. Would you mind watching the baby while I do a little shopping?" "No, honey, I can't be a room mother this year with two babies in diapers." Let your life be genuine.

- Have realistic expectations of yourself and others. Often we get into trouble because we expect too much of ourselves. Set some realistic limits on what you try to accomplish in a day. Try to accept others as they are, not as you wish they were.

- Look on the interests of others. Depression tends to make me focus on my needs. And perhaps that's part of the work of depression. If you become depressed through burnout, you may need to take better care of yourself and your needs. Be careful though because a "me-centered" world gets awfully small.

If we aren't careful, our mates will begin to feel that no matter what they do, we stay depressed. Depression can become contagious and pretty soon the whole house has the plague.

You will find yourself much happier if you begin to look on the interests of your family. Don't be afraid they will take advantage of you. As long as you are honest in letting them know your needs, you will be safe in meeting theirs and giving them kindnesses. My husband was helping with the laundry, the house-keeping, the baby and older children, buying groceries, while trying to be president of a bank. And I'm sorry to say, I don't think I even realized his sacrifices.

- Give up guilt, and move on. (See Ch. 11 "Forgiving God, Self, and others") We all make mistakes in life. I may feel guilty for a mistake I've made or for letting my family down but hanging on to guilt prevents me from the normal give and take of marriage and family. Some of the best things we learn come from our mistakes. Picture yourself as a two-year-old. Does a two-year-old always walk well? Of course not, he stumbles, falls, picks himself up and toddles along. God knows we will make mistakes and fall down. Humpty needs to get up and try again. Pray that God will bring good out of your present distress. He never wastes anything.

- Ground yourself in the Word of God. The scriptures are full of comfort, encouragement, correction, and instruction. St. Paul tells husbands and wives to "submit to one another out of the love of Christ" (Ephesians Ch. 5:21). I need to submit my best thoughts and ideas even if I have lost confidence in myself. In a marriage, God gives wisdom to both partners.

  Although out mates may find it uncomfortable to listen to our feelings or to let us experience emotions, it is important to let them into our thinking. I never shared my feelings of worry about relocating. I remembered my grandfather, educated at Notre Dame, working as a blacksmith in a small community because grandma had too much fear to live where he could have used his education. I wanted my husband to achieve his dreams and goals so I buried my concerns and did not let him know how lonely I felt when we moved. I know he didn't realize he walked into an environment waiting for him. I felt I had to start at ground zero. I'm sure I missed the encouragement and understanding he could have given me.

  I didn't realize that sharing my fears would help George to "know" me. If your mate isn't open to you sharing these feelings, share them with a trustworthy friend.

- Develop a sense of humor. Don't make mountains out of molehills. Don't take yourself so seriously.

Put a little fun in your life. The first thing our daughter Jodie did when she would arrive from the city at our lake retreat was to let out a big mountain type yell. I am married to a serious, no-nonsense executive but I began to wake up singing a little off key song, or a special Tarzan yodel. His first reaction was to "shush" me. He would often say, "What will the neighbors think or people can hear you for ten miles." But secretly he liked it because it was so off the wall. One of the girls got him the "singing fish" and he began to get up and push the "Don't worry be happy" verse or "Take me to the Water." Marriage needs a little fun.

A friend was married to a serious type also. She had purchased one of my little bears dressed in drapery material at a church bazaar. One evening when my husband and I were visiting, the couple began to tell us about the antics of the little bear. On one occasion my friend found the little bear hanging from a ceiling fan. Another time, she found the little bear behind the bedroom door with a pile of raisins beside it. Or she might find it, (glasses perched on its nose) on top the bed reading a book. She even brought it to a barbecue as a hippy with a bandana and earring. But the best story was the night Liz got in the car dressed formally for a dinner dance and turned to see the little bear sitting in the backseat of the car with a small fur stole and diamond (?) earrings. We need to make our marriages more fun.

Since I tend to be the church-involved type, I decided we needed a special date that was non-religion oriented. I call these dates "mystery date." On one of the first dates, I told my husband to put on a suit and tie, I was taking him someplace special. He wasn't sure he wanted to take the risk. I told him he would have to trust me. I asked a couple of our friends to join us and the other husband drove. The idea was that George would be totally surprised. By the time we got to the "dinner train," George had guessed our destination. Other dates placed us at musicals, plays, nice restaurants… all places I hoped he would enjoy.

In depression, it's important to check our relationships not only with our mates but with our children, bosses, and those close to us. Unhealthy or unhappy relationships can be one of the underlying causes of depression.

In working with small women's Bible studies and prayer groups through the years, I have noticed a prevalent cause of chronic depression—women who attend church alone and aren't sure where their husbands are in regard to spiritual matters.

These women had a passion to know God, to understand His thoughts through study of the bible, to walk a Christian walk, and to become more spiritual. Many times their husbands immersed in the world trying to earn a living and provide financial security for their families, would not have the same desire for Christian growth. Though these men loved their wives, I suspect they thought their wives were not living in the real world and wished they would be more concerned for the everyday practical aspects of life. We can become a little obsessed with religious activities.

Many of the women attended church alone. They buried themselves in Christian work, and prayed for years that their mates would come to know God as they did and that they would be able to share their faith and concerns with their husband.

There were times when my husband had so much responsibility at work and so many home projects that he did not attend church. I remember driving the children to Sunday School and joining an ongoing Bible study or women's study, (rather than drive 30 min. home and return). Once a couple who were leaders in the church greeted me and then said, "Where is your husband?" It was a terrible feeling. A feeling of being on the outside.

If you are in a marriage situation where your husband or wife is not as on fire for spiritual things as you are, remember that they may feel you have joined a Christian country club without them. Using a Christian vocabulary can also alienate them making them feel like they are on the outside.

There is a difference in being a Christian and being religious. Religion is legalistic (has mega rules), can be unloving, and is exclusive. Walking with God, reading his Word and putting it into your life, making the two great commandments your way of life, ("Love the Lord your God with your whole heart, and mind and soul and your neighbor as yourself") produce a different life. In the gospels we find Jesus accepting people as they are, giving them unconditional love, and setting an example for them to follow. We would be wise to imitate Jesus.

If you are depressed because you don't know how to live your life married to someone who doesn't have this passion for the Lord, I would share this reminder.

In (Matthew Ch. 20: 1-16), the landowner hires hands for the work of the day. He hires the first people early in the morning, some at mid-day and others shortly before the end of the day. If God calls you to follow Him at 6 a.m. and does not call your mate until 6 p.m. that is His choice. God's walk with each person is private. He is the potter. Our job is to love and make sure the log is out of our own eye.

Jesus reminds us that no one knows hearts except God. Our job is to love not to judge. When we slip into an accusatory mind (judging and unloving), we do not represent the unconditional love of Christ. Leave your loved ones in the hands of God through prayer and concentrate on making love your passion.

In Chapter 1 we discussed personality. Personality plays a big role in the balance of the teeter-totter. Opposites attract. Many times a popular people person will be married to a quiet, conservative; an organized mover and shaker to an easy-going Lily. Has one personality in a marriage become more powerful and self-assured? This will skew the teeter-totter.

How we are able to support a loved one who is depressed will also depend on our personality type. If I am a "Mum" I won't be able to figure out why my mate doesn't just get up and get going. If I am a Sunflower, I will get depressed living with depression. I need life to be more fun. I won't be attracted to my mate's personal pity parties. (I can say this since I was the depressed person.) I'll do better at comfort and caring if I'm a Lily. And if I'm a Rose, I may just catch the depression virus since I need a lot of special attention myself which I won't be getting from my partner.

Mutual respect and concern balance the teeter-totter. Because my husband was so capable and organized, I began to feel inadequate in my own roles. I needed to find some area that he was not more gifted than I. Risking beginning (I had to be willing to start something I knew nothing about.) I joined watercolor classes and began making quilts. The first quilt I completed, the first painting that sold, gave me a feeling of self worth and enabled my husband to be proud of me again.

At some point, we who have given up the duty need to reclaim our responsibilities and do them "as unto the Lord." I found when I made this switch, I stopped comparing my ability to my husband's.

Power, money, and success embolden people. One summer, I met several lovely women who had finished raising their children but seemed to have lost their "mission." Four of them were on antidepressants, Their husbands, on the other hand, were retired self-assured, successful CEO's, judges, lawyers, dentists, businessmen who had grown strong through the years.

What happened in these marriages? The self-assured took control. These women needed new goals, a purpose for their lives. Grandchildren can help fill the gap but they needed to begin new lives, developing new skills, interests, or hobbies. God has good plans for each season of our lives.

It is difficult to sit on the teeter-totter with a person who has taken control. Like the little "father bear" he may sit with his feet firmly planted on the ground watching you struggle to stay on board. If you are married to a controlling man, or woman, begin to own your life. It does belong to you. Use gentle "I" statements to let your partner know when he has crossed the line. "Honey, I love you but it hurts my feelings when you talk to me as if I'm a child." They may be unaware that their manner has changed.

One summer we stopped to visit a friend of my husband's. We hadn't seen this gentleman in many years. He had been a quiet man who was sincere and helpful. He and his wife invited us to stay overnight. We haven't seen them since. Their hospitality was lovely but the change my husband saw in his boyhood friend was too much. He had reached a position of power in a large company and the power had changed his personality. His wife waited on him but seemed intimidated. He had become a different person.

There are boundaries that sometimes need to be drawn. Here are a few I've heard used by women friends:

If you aren't allowed to have conversation when your mate is watching television you might say, "Is it all right to talk now, I don't want to interrupt something important you are trying to watch."

People with strong opinions which are well thought out may not understand their mate having a different point-of-view. Sometimes, they just need to hear, "What a good idea; or sounds reasonable to me." But if you have an opinion you really want to share, don't hesitate. We need to respect the fact that others may hold different beliefs.

Dr. Carter and Dr. Minirth in their book.[4] The Freedom From Depression Workbook give some warnings to people with a controller in their life—(there is only one way—my way.) When you learn what triggers your boss, mother, father, or mate, you may manage your life so you don't press those buttons. You in essence, control yourself. The bottom line is, you are still controlled. Beware.

---

[4]   Les Carter, PhD, Frank Martin, MD *The Freedom from Depression Workbook*, Ch. 7 'Finding Release from Control," Thomas Nelson, Nashville.

In Chapter 7 of the Minirth workbook, the authors warn us not to live our lives to please a person but to live our lives to please God. He is the only One worthy of worship. If you let another take power, you give up your freedom of choice. The imperative person makes all the choices for you. Even well meaning individuals can have such strong opinions, so well articulated that you are unable to be who you really are. One of the older members in our family read magazine articles on health and became the family authority on medical subjects; yet, I had a B.S. in Nursing. Another relative gave financial advice, yet, my husband had been president of two large banks.

As we observe nature we see that God not only created hawks and eagles, He created sparrows and hummingbirds. And the song of the sparrow is lovely. Don't let anyone still your song. In the following story, Florence Littauer illustrates an occasion in her family when lack of encouragement almost stilled her father's song.[5]

(Paraphrase) Shortly before he died, Florence's father called her into the small bedroom behind their butcher shop and handed her a cigar box full of clippings. Florence found newspaper and magazine articles and a personal letter from an important political figure. She was puzzled. Why had her father saved these particular articles?

Then Florence saw it-the author's name was her own dear father whom she thought was a butcher. He told her he wanted to be a writer but his wife, a practical woman, advised him this was impossible; he wasn't an educated man. So, he wrote in secret. No one knew he was a published

---

[5]   Florence Littauer, Silver Boxes, The Encouragement Book, Word Publishing, My 1990. (p. 124,125)

author. How different her father's life might have been if he had been encouraged, his opinions valued.

Working for a difficult boss may cause a person to sink into depression. Our daughters had this experience:

One girl's boss thought he was god. He was loud, rude, and verbally abusive. He made promises which he didn't keep concerning salaries and benefits. In five years working for this boss, she received almost no encouragement often feeling totally intimidated.

Every night, she left work relieved she had made it through another day. At one point, she knew she had to leave this negative environment even though jobs were scarce in her field and she needed to be able to pay her bills.

Another boss, was unreliable, dishonest, and broke his promises. He literary couldn't keep people working for him because of his temperament. Our daughter found herself doing three or four people's jobs—a good way to learn business but terrible on the health. She came to a point where, job at risk, she met with her boss and confronted him about his attitude and behavior. She told him she would always work hard and do her best but she expected respect. Like her sister, she needed a salary to pay her bills.

- **Try to set limits or boundaries.** It may be difficult to know when to "turn the other cheek" and when to hold the destructive person accountable. You may stand up for yourself by using "I" statements like, "Sir, you will always get a hundred percent from me but… I need to be treated in a respectful way."

- **Polite Confrontation**. The imperative boss is King of the beast. He senses weakness and insecurity. His natural instincts cause him to treat each person according to the strength he senses. He gives respect and space to the strong, but is deaf and abusive to the weak. You have little power to change him, but when you show courage, he may back down.

- **Have a back-up plan.** What's the worst case scenario? No job. How would you pay your bills? Try to save a couple of month's rent, house payment—be prepared. Prepare a resume. Keep your ear alert for other opportunities. If you are in danger of losing your physical, mental or spiritual health, then take the Biblical directive "Flee evil." God doesn't approve of this kind of abuse.

Pray that God will help you shed verbal abuse like the oil on a duck's back. Try not to take undeserved criticism to heart. It's really their problem, not yours.

I have a "morale booster" for when my self-esteem is low. I collect pictures of outrageous women which I call "You Go Girl" pictures. As the old saying goes, a picture is worth a thousand words. The first picture is of an old Russian woman, scarf over her head, leaning into a powerful walk—a woman on a mission; the second is an old woman with white hair, colorful clothing who is sitting on a step smoking a big cigar—enough said; the third addition is a picture of a 94 year-old-woman, frail and tiny, riding six miles a day on a very large tricycle. These pictures make me smile and say to me, "You go, girl."

If you are in an unbalanced marriage, or in a work situation where your teeter-totter is skewed, God will strengthen you and lead you day by day.

Memorize verses like:

- "in God I trust; I will not be afraid. What can mortal man do to me? (Psalm 56:3,4)

- "Greater is He who is within (me) than he who is in the world" (1 John 4:4)

- "I can do all things in Christ who strengthens me. (Philippians Ch. 4:13.)

The Holy Spirit, the Comforter and Strengthener, will give Humpty the backbone to balance the teeter-totter. Be calm and firm! Take a deep breath. And if you can't straighten out this relationship alone, seek a Christian counselor or pastor. Review the words of this favorite prayer:

Serenity Prayer

God grant me the
SERENITY
To accept the things
I cannot change,
COURAGE
To change the things I can,
WISDOM
To know the difference
(source unknown)

Chapter 10

Examining Key Relationships

1. Consider your most important relationships:

Mate:
Parents:
Children:
Boss

2. On a basis of 1-5 with 5 being balanced, how would you rate each of the above relationships? Is the teeter-totter balanced?

3. When you are upset with one of the above, which statement best shows your approach.

    a. I let it go and just push my feelings down.
    b. I challenge. "You acted like a..."
    c. I state my feelings, "I want you to know that when you speak to me in that tone, I feel like a non-person."

4. Look up the following verses. What suggestion does the verse have for communication?

James 1:19
Colossians 3:12, 13
Philippians 4:13
Philippians 4:5
Philippians 2:4
Ephesians 4:15

5. What does setting boundaries mean to you?

6. Prayer for wisdom and strength.

Dear Heavenly Father, I feel confused. I don't know if you want me to confront hurtful behavior or let it go. Help me to have the wisdom and understanding to change my response to poor treatment. Lord, you are my strength and you are my backbone. Protect me and guide me so that I may walk in truth and love. I ask this in Jesus' name. Amen.

Forgiving God, Self, Others

"And be kind to one another, tenderhearted, forgiving each other, just as God in Christ also has forgiven you."
(Ephesians 4:32)

Forgive forever

Others, self and God

Release resentment

Grapple with grudges

Initiate new beginnings

Vengeance is God's

Erase anger, Enact love.

S.Burke

Forgive God, Self, and Others

"Father forgive them; for they do not
know what they are doing."
(Luke Ch. 23:34)

"Daddy will never forgive me," three-year-old Lindsay sobbed, tears running down her face. "He wouldn't talk to me, Mommy. Will he talk to me?"

Mommy knelt down beside her. "Are you sorry for hurting brother, Lindsay?"

"Yes."

"Can you ask him to forgive you?"

"Will you forgive me, Matthew?" Lindsay said.

Matthew, the five-year-old gentleman brother mumbled. "Okay, I guess so."

Then Lindsay repeated her foremost concern, "but will Daddy ever forgive me?" Daddy had refused to talk to her on the telephone because Lindsay, eager to tell her adventures, had scratched Matthew so he dropped the phone. Daddy was using tough love.

"Lindsay," continued mother, "Daddy will forgive you, but you must not hurt Matthew again. Jesus tells us to always forgive. Can you ask Jesus to forgive you?"

"Please Jesus, forgive me," Lindsay prayed. "Help me to be good."

On occasion, we need to start over with God, ourselves and other. Is there a mistake in your past that haunts you—a failed marriage, a child out of wedlock, an abortion, a stint of heroin abuse, a path which ruined or changed your life forever? Is there someone you hurt, or someone who hurt you so deeply that you no longer have peace? No longer have God.

Recently, a neighbor dropped by. She saw I had a dress on and wondered where I was going. Casual attire is the norm in our small mountain community. I smiled. "I like to wear a dress when I go to church," I said. She looked away. "Do you have a church?" I asked.

"I used to have one until I was divorced." She hesitated. "My church doesn't allow divorce. When I remarried,…"

Are there sins that are unforgivable? My neighbor thought so. She felt she'd moved outside God's love.

The Bible tells us a different story. King David committed adultery and murder; yet, God said he was a "man after his own heart." How could that be?

Reading Psalm 51:1-4, we hear David cry out to God, "have mercy on me, O God, according to your unfailing love; according to your great compassion blot out my transgressions. Wash away all my iniquity and cleanse me from my sin. For I know my transgressions, and my sin is always before me. Against you, you only, have I sinned and done what is evil in your sight, so that you are proved right when you speak and justified when you judge…" In (v. 10) he says, "Create in me a pure heart, O God, and renew a steadfast spirit within me. Do not cast me from your presence or take your Holy Spirit from me." Did God forgive him? Yes, but the consequences of David's actions followed him. His child with Bathsheba died shortly after birth. His adulterous behavior set a terrible model which his sons followed.

God loves us. He forgives even the most heinous sin when the heart is sorry and as proof, He sent his only son to pay the price for our sins. Jesus dies for our forgiveness. It is there for all of us. We don't have to live our lives without God because our actions put us outside of God's love. We have grace.

At three, Lindsay, whose middle name is Grace, was already learning this. In her toddler way, she knew that she didn't want to be without her father's love. She wanted Daddy to talk to her again.

My daughter, using the principle found in (1 John 1:9) "If we confess our sins, He is faithful and just and will forgive us our sins and purify us from all unrighteousness," guided her well. "Do you want to ask Jesus to forgive you, honey?" We need only ask. Simply ask.

A second step Lindsay models is to go to the one you have injured and ask them to forgive you. Matthew, still smarting from Lindsay's fingernails on his bare back, hesitated; he had to think it over; but in the end, he forgave Lindsay. God tells us to make things right with those we have injured, if it is possible (not possible if they have died or will not allow us to ask forgiveness.)

Many years ago, I felt bad chemistry every time I was with one of my relatives. Yet, I couldn't remember doing anything to offend her. Praying, I felt compelled to go see this woman. I dreaded going. I called her and asked if I could pay her a visit. She was surprised, but invited me to come by. At her invitation, I sat down. "I don't know if I have offended you in some way or hurt your feelings, but if I have, I would like to ask you to forgive me," I said.

She became quiet; my apology was unexpected. Then she began to pour out the hurt that had built up in her heart through the years. Careless words had triggered a personal offense. She viewed me as an enemy.

I reiterated my apology telling her I hoped we could start again. In spite of repeated kind words and actions on my part, years went by before I regained this person's trust. Forgiveness doesn't always follow a sincere apology.

If I am the guilty party, like Lindsay, I need to have a "heart to heart" with the Lord asking His forgiveness. Once this is accomplished, <u>I need to forgive myself.</u> Holding memorials over past mistakes prevents me from enjoying the peace God has for me. I must forget what lies behind; today is all I have.

Guilt often blocks my ability to love myself. Is that important? Jesus taught us to love the Lord our God with our whole heart, mind, and soul and to love our neighbor *as ourselves.* Many depressed people do not love themselves. We have failed to live up to others' expectations. We see failure in the mirror.

John Powell, S.J. in his book *Happiness Is An Inside Job,*[6] makes this statement, "We must first love ourselves... to the extent that I fail to love myself, to that extent I will be unable to love others.

Powell tells us that if we grow up without feeling loved and safe, we will trust no one. Because we have never felt real love and acceptance, we will be unable to accept and love ourselves-we'll always feel starved for affection and attention and never satisfied with love that is given. A person starved for love simply doesn't know how to take love in. The point

---

[6]   John Powell, S.J. *Happiness Is An Inside Job,*

is, if I never experience love and safety as a child, I will live in a shrunken world of one unable to trust God or man for I have no idea of what trust is. Powell goes on to say, "The source of most chronic unhappiness is a failure to love."

Check 1 Corinthians Ch. 13 asking yourself these questions: Am I patient with myself? Am I kind to myself? Do I forgive myself? Do I hope good things for myself? Am I too sensitive about myself? Do I judge myself too critically? Do the answers to these questions show that I love and accept myself? I begin by asking God for forgiveness, accepting it and starting over. Humpty needs to love herself, so she can love others.

Has someone injured me so deeply, the hurt still haunts me? Like a grain of sand irritates the oyster, does this wound lay hidden in my heart irritating and producing the poison of anger and resentment? Unlike the grain of sand in the oyster's shell that produces a pearl, my grain will only produce an abscess in the soul and ulcers in my stomach.

How do I let go of the anger and hurt? What do I do when resentment keeps popping its ugly head up?

Try journaling. Write down the entire episode or episodes. Don't leave out any details. State your feelings, the injury, your anger, and resentment. Then tear up the pages and bury it in your garbage can or burn it. The act of getting rid of bad thoughts helps make forgiveness real.

As a gardener, I've learned that I can't always get rid of an unwanted plant. I've removed the main roots but sometimes tiny roots send shoots to the surface. This can happen when we try to forgive. When these feelings reoccur, go to Jesus and ask him to remove these new roots of anger or resentment. This is a natural process and doesn't mean you haven't forgiven.

Did anyone injure Jesus and not ask forgiveness? Yes, Jesus was beaten, cursed, mocked, and eventually nailed to a cross. Did he strike down His accusers? Did He call the myriad of angels to wipe them off the face of the earth? No. He said, "Father forgive them for they know not what they do."

Joseph is another example of one who was mistreated (Genesis Ch. 39-45). His brothers hated him. They put Joseph into a pit and abandoned him. He went from the rich man's son to a slave in a foreign culture.

We hear no complaints from Joseph as he serves as a slave, is accused, and goes to prison. What is his outcome? Joseph, is called before Pharaoh to interpret a dream. He tells Pharaoh there will be seven good years followed by seven years of famine. He counsels Pharaoh to store grain in the good years to carry Egypt through the bad years. Pharaoh puts Joseph in charge of the plan and he becomes second only to Pharaoh.

Later Joseph's brother come before him. These are the words he say to the brothers who mistreated him. "Do not be distressed and do not be angry with yourselves for selling me here, because it was to save lives that God sent me ahead of you." (vs. 8) "So then, it was not you who sent me here, but God…" (Genesis Ch. 45:5-8)

God protected Joseph. He taught Joseph management skills while he was a slave in Potiphar's house. Joseph would need these skills when he later became second in command of Egypt. Cast into prison, Joseph was put in charge of the other prisoners. He developed humility and caring for others. God wastes nothing in our lives. And in His time, He takes all things that happens to us, not just some things, but all things and uses them to good for those who love Him and are called by His name.

Harboring hatred, anger and resentment produce the acid soil for a bitter root. Instead of holding these destructive feelings, can we follow the example of Jesus and Joseph and let our righteous anger go? Could we pray every day for a month for the person who hurt us, perform an act of kindness, or send a note of encouragement? In this way, we can exchange death for life.

The third category is forgiving the Lord. We ask, how could He have allowed... why didn't He send an angel to protect? Where was God when my daughter was raped? How can a good God stand by and let evil have its way? We are angry with God.

If God is so powerful, why didn't He intervene or go ahead to protect us, we reason. We may never have the answer. The Bible says "Give thanks to the Lord, for He is good. His love endures forever. (Psalm 136 vs. I). It states there is no darkness on Him (I John 1:5) If He is good, we must trust Him even when we don't understand.

Earthly fathers aren't always good. Perhaps, they aren't concerned about us, or abuse us. God is our heavenly Father; we can count on Him.

I know that He is all good, all wise, all knowing; there is no darkness or evil in God. He is for us, not against us; He has good plans for our lives. And yet, into each life the rain will fall. Remember, it rains on the good and the bad. God is able to handle our questions. We can trust Him.

"Lord, my heart is broken. How could you allow this to happen? Why didn't you tell me? But even now, O Lord I trust you to make something good out of my suffering, and my life. It is my gift to you. Lord, forgive me for doubting your goodness. Amen."

The roots of depression may be entwined in unforgiveness. Put it under God's microscope. Take the steps of forgiveness and follow the creed in this prayer:

"Lord, make me an instrument of your peace.
Where there is hatred, let me sow love.
Where there is injury, pardon;
Where there is doubt, faith;
Where there is despair, hope
And where there is sadness, joy."

Prayer of St. Francis of Assisi

Chapter 11

Forgiving God, Self, and Others

Exercises: Read Psalm 51

1. Is there a sin you need to ask God to forgive? Have you hurt someone? Do you need to ask their forgiveness?

2. Is there a person who has hurt you deeply? Write every memory of this person and the hurt. Get it off your mind.

*   Tear the writing into little pieces. Burn them in a fireplace.
*   Pray for the person who hurt you.
*   Pray that God will wipe away painful memories.

3. Think of some kind act you could do for that person:

*   Send an anonymous card
*   Pray a simple prayer for them every day for a week.

4. Read 1 Corinthians Ch. 13- the love chapter. Insert your own name in each thought. Am I patient with myself?

5. Make the prayer of St. Francis of Assisi your mission. When someone hurts you, forgive them.

Friends for Comfort and Counsel

"A friend is someone who knows the song
in your heart and can sing it back to you
when you have forgotten the words."
(Unknown)

Humpty Dumpty sat on a wall
Humpty Dumpty had a great fall…

Then Humpty torn apart, strung out, disembodied, does a strange thing. Instead of getting himself together, he begins rebuilding the wall. He positions himself behind the wall, protected by it. Humpty will take no chances. He learned from his fall that risk is costly. To Humpty it is not better to have loved and lost. It is better to protect himself from the chance of failure or hurt. He is safe behind the wall.

In the last two chapters, we have looked at our relationship with people and God. We have asked both God and man to forgive us and we have said we need to forgive those who have injured us. Depression seems to cause isolation. Like our nursery rhyme Humpty, some of us who fall off the wall want to take no more chances. We won't become visible or vulnerable nor will we risk rejection from anyone. The world had its chance to know us and blew it. If we walk again, we will wear our armor to protect our fragile shells.

I may actually build a wall of fat around me—a flesh wall. I may become hardened, callused or untouchable.

Perhaps, I will withdraw and become reclusive. Is this the right road to take? At the end of this road will there be a rainbow and a pot of gold?

NO!

We need help. May I suggest if you are depressed, go against your natural inclination and reach out. Stay in a small supportive group—a Sunday school class, or even a card club, or a golf foursome.

When depressed, I'm not a good friend. I'm not fun to be with so I won't be the first one picked to go to a luncheon. But the most important thing I have to say about friends in depression is you *won't get well without one or more*. God, the Holy Spirit, living in our hearts will begin to draw the people He wants into our lives.

A Heart Friend If you have a heart friend who loves you and won't let you alone, you are a blessed person. Michael W. Smith wrote about this kind of friendship in his song *Friends*. "Friends are friends forever" is an old-fashioned idea but difficult in our transient society. My own depression was worsened because we were living in a new town, with no friends, family or church.

Mike Wallace confessed on television that at one period in his life he was so depressed he was suicidal. Every night, no matter where he was, his friend Art Buckwald called to encourage him. Someone knew; someone cared. The Spirit may assign a part-time friend, one to do a special task. Be on the lookout for these special God-sent friends. They have a mission. God has sent them especially to you.

*A friend **Who Listens*** will give you an opportunity to pour your heart out. She should be confidential and trustworthy. She won't have the answers. She is not your savior but she will listen and care. You can confess your deep pain, sin, or hurt. She will be there for you to tell it like it is. She must be sent by God.

*A friend **Who Is A Prayer Warrior*** These are rare people who walk closely with the Lord. When they pray, things happen. Peace cover your heart. Their job is to lift your burdens and put them in the hands of the Lord. In the Old Testament, Moses became a prayer warrior for the people of God. The people were fighting a strong enemy, the Amalekites. Moses went up on the mountain and prayed to God lifting his arms to heaven. As long as Moses arms were raised in prayer, the Israelites won the battle. When Moses arms grew tired and he lowered his arms, the people lost. All of us have difficult periods in our lives. We need others to pray and lift their arms to heaven on our behalf. The prayer warrior stands guard while you rebuild your life.

*A friend **who walks alongside**-* This special friend accepts you as is. She calls you, writes you email, sends you little gifts, comes over to see how you are. She is an encourager focusing you on God's love, His power, His good plans for your life. She doesn't give up on you, but is persistent in her friendship.

*A friend **who has walked where you are walking**-* If the Lord sends this friend she will serve you as a mentor. She will share her own story and how she worked through it with the Lord. Based on 11 Corinthians Ch. 1 vs. 3-6, she comforts you with the comfort and wisdom God comforted her with. *She will know how your walk is without* *you saying anything.* If you are a new widow, she is an older widow. If you are newly diagnosed of cancer, she has had surgery, chemotherapy, etc. If you are taking care of an Alzheimer's patient, she will have walked that road and have many suggestions to help you. She will give you the gift of understanding and compassion.

A friend who keeps me accountable- This friend is able to gently tell you when your thoughts or attitudes are out of order, too negative, or destructive. Listen to this friend. If she challenges your thoughts, heart attitudes or isolation, respond to what she tells you. She can be your reality check, a walking discipline in your life. God may use her to correct you; if so, don't be hurt. She is a valuable friend.

A friend who brings Chicken soup- This friend literally brings you soup, or soup for the soul in the form of prayers, devotional material, uplifting books. She tries to get your mind on things that are beautiful, lovely, of good repute. She may offer to take you to a concert, an art show, an interesting play, or to hear a special Christian speaker. She may want you to join a Bible study or go to church with her. She is your Chicken Soup friend.

A friend who lifts your mood- This angel makes you feel good. She is positive and energizes you with hope. Her contribution may just be to insert a little fun in your life, to take you to lunch, lighten the load, interest you in the world again.

The professional friend- If you are a very private person, you may not wish to confide intimately in a personal friend. You might find it easier to talk to a professional who has confidentiality codes. A psychiatrist, psychologist, counselor, social worker, psychiatric nurse, minister, or doctor are the professional friend. Choose well.

The American Association of Christian Counselors has 44,000 qualified counselors with impeccable credentials. You can reach their website at www.AACC.net for suggestions of qualified counselors in your area. These professionals are Christians whom God has gifted in the "help and encouragement" ministry. They will pray for you and counsel you according to Biblical principles. They can help you with relationships, and guide you in the beginning a new life.

Chuck Noon, Christian, counselor in the Albuquerque, NM area encourages us to interview prospective therapists. Ask for their education credentials. Was the counselor's program accredited by the American Association for Marriage and Family Therapy?

A nurse who was a friend of mine, became depressed after she quit working and retired. Her psychiatrist could not find a drug which worked well for her. He finally recommended she go to a psychologist who had just opened a practice. She was told he used the latest techniques to help people. She learned biofeedback but the psychologists wanted her to let him regress her to a former life where he was sure her troubles started. At this point, my friend quit going to the psychologist.

A daughter of another friend received her doctorate in psychology and opened a private practice. I visited her waiting room which was decorated to look like someone's living room. Soft, relaxing music was playing. Chicken Soup and other inspirational books were placed in the waiting room for her clients to read instead of magazines. So far so good.

When I interviewed her and asked what her specialty was, she handed me a card which identified herself as a channeler. A channeler contacts spirits from the dead to help with the problems of this world. She also hypnotized patients and regressed them to other lives. She had mixed Christianity and the occult.

God gives clear instructions in Deuteronomy 18 as to his thoughts on using Tarot cards, crystal gazing, mediums— (channelers), studying the stars (horoscopes) and having séances. (Deutoronomy Ch. 18:9-14).

"When you enter the land the Lord your God is giving you, do not learn to imitate the detestable ways of the nations. Let no one be found among you who... practices divination (forecasting the future by the study of the stars-astrology or horoscopes), or sorcery, interprets omens, engages in witchcraft, or casts spells or who is a medium (channeler) or spiritists or who consults the dead. Anyone who does these things is detestable to the Lord."

This is why I said choose well. Get a counselor who holds the same belief system you do and will respect the ways of God according to the Bible.

The greatest friend, The Lord Jesus. The Lord can make your telephone ring. He can get you the right video teaching series or book to help you take the next step. He will send any number of the above friends to be your encouragers. Draw near to Him and He will draw near to you.

Most of us won't have one friend who will do all these areas for us. God often appoints one of these short-term friends with a small mission just when we need them. Look for them. Accept the gift of friendship they bring.

Family can often be the friends who encourage us. A special bond exists in families. As a family, our six children and spouses surround one another with prayers, love and encouragement. If you have a dysfunctional family, or one who does not know God, He will send you other friends to pray and encourage you.

Depression feels like you have fallen into a dark pit. You need someone to open the window and let in the light or to throw you a rope so you have a way to climb out. It is a prison. Perhaps, the 30,000,000 people in depression would not be there if they had a friend to reach out and give them a hand up.

Even Jesus needed friends. The night before he was crucified, He took Peter, James and John up the mountain while he prayed. He needed them to support Him in prayer but unknowing the future, they fell asleep exhausted. I hope each person who needs a friend finds one who is awake!

Several years ago, I discovered a Mexican sculpture made of clay. It was entitled "The Crossbearers." A dozen Mexican children held a cross on their shoulders. All the children helped to carry the cross. The sculpture speaks more eloquently than any words.

Depressed people need friends to walk alongside and help them carry their cross. We won't make it without you!

Humpty must not climb behind her wall. She needs to open her heart and allow God to send his love through people. We need to allow others to befriend us and when we are able, to become a friend to someone else.

Thank you to some of my special friends along life's way: Liz, Patty, Phyllis, Carol, Michele, Marta, Margie, Sally, Peg, Connie, Rose, Jewell and Arlene!

Chapter 12

Friends for Comfort and Counsel

Exercises:

1. Pray for a special wise counselor, someone who has been where you are.

2. Bible study: Read the story of David's friendship with Saul's son, Jonathan. How was Jonathan a good friend to David? (1 Samuel Ch. 18 thru Ch. 20)

3. List the most important qualities of a friend.

4. Are you part of any small group? A Bible study? A sports' team? A bridge club? A Sunday school class? If not, consider joining a group of people with the same interests. Isolation is part of depression.

5. Could you use a professional friend? Remember the website www.aacc.net.

6. If you do not have a habit of reading the Bible, challenge yourself to read one chapter a day. A good place to begin is the Gospel of John. Reading the Word of God will help Jesus speak to you.

7. Make a 3 by 5 card for any verse which seems to stand out each day. File in a file box by subject for quick reference. (Fear, anxiety, thankfulness).

V. A Healthy Body

Can Medicine Help?

"Plans fail for lack of counsel, but with many
advisers they succeed." (Proverbs 15:22)

How can medicine best serve us in depression? Our
family doctors, internists, and HMO's can be on the alert
for depression when administering annual physicals.

Dr. Harold Bloomfield, MD and Peter McWilliams
authored a classic article in Good Housekeeping that lays
out a simple method for physicians and psychiatrists to
use in evaluating a patient.[7] According to these doctors,
many patients show up in the doctor's office with insomnia,
fatigue, anxiety, stress, and vague aches and pains. Dr.
Bloomfield outlines his approach to an individual whose
complaints may include the symptoms described above.

1. Patient gives a medical history—Does depression
   run in the family?

2. Medical workup. Check for: low thyroid, hepatitis,
   mono-nucleosis, anemia, diabetes, Alzheimer's
   disease—diseases known to cause depression.

3. What medications is the person taking? (Certain
   drugs given for high blood pressure such as reserpine
   may precipitate depression. Other drugs, some birth

---

[7] Dr. Harold Bloomfield, M.D. and Peter McWilliams, *"New
Hope New Help for Depression,"* Good Housekeeping v. 219,
p.58, Aug 94.

control pills, major tranquilizers, valium, Ritalin can have a depressant effect.)

4. Furnish a complete list of vitamins, minerals, herbs, amino acids taken in the past year.

5. Talk to the patient. In her own words, what are her symptoms? What is bringing her into the doctor?

Blood chemistry is checked for low mineral content, thyroid levels, anemia etc.

In a complete physical, the doctor keeps in mind the effect of pregnancy, childbirth, menopause knowing hormonal changes may signal depression. Changes in estrogen levels play havoc with our chemistry.

A complete physical also includes mammography if age appropriate, a Pap smear, (and in a post menopausal woman, an evaluation of estrogen replacement therapy and osteoporosis.)

The doctor evaluates nutrition. What am I eating? I may be instructed to write down my entire diet for one or two weeks.

If the doctor discovers depression symptoms, catching them early, he may be in a position to head off severe depression. At this point, the physician may treat or refer me to a psychiatrist a counselor, or pastor.

The psychiatrist has several roles:

1. Assesses the degree of depression. Does the patient need hospitalizing? Is she nonfunctioning, suicidal, or a danger to others?

2. Plans a course of treatment.

3. Evaluates the use of herbal mood elevators, amino acids, or antidepressant therapy, to change chemicals and increase serotonin.

4. Determines whether patient would benefit from counseling or psychotherapy. May refer to a social worker, counselor, clergy or begin psychotherapy himself.

Research is showing the good effects of prayer on health. Man is not just mind and body but is created with a spirit. Usually, the psychiatrist uses a two-pronged treatment: mood-elevating drugs, and talk therapy. In reality, not everyone has faith in God. Professionals must respect the beliefs a person comes to them with but as patients seeking care we can try to choose a physician or psychiatrist whose beliefs line up with our own. What would happen if as patients we asked to begin our counseling sessions with prayer asking God to provide wisdom?

Marianne Szegedy-Maszak in her article "The career of a celebrity pill" U.S. News and World Report, August 6, 2001, refers to a dissatisfaction developing in the psychiatric community about using drug therapy alone. She states, "Harvard psychiatrist David Osser acknowledges that mental disorders are in part brain disorders and can be ameliorated in the same way as, say, a liver disorder. But the brain is not and will never be just another organ, he insists, for the simple reason that the mind resides there." Osser further states, "the understanding of the mind, and how it operates-how we think and acquire our values-may be beyond science.

Ms. Szegeby-Maszak states that these drugs don't always work for everyone. "Even when they work initially, they sometimes lose their potency with regular use…" Although these drugs are hard to overdose on, withdrawal from their use can be severe.[8]

In 2015 the New York Times stated that 30,000,000 Americans were known to be on antidepressant therapy, one out of four women age 40-50. Global research reports that this is a multi-billion dollar industry.

At present, five types of antidepressants are on the market. The psychiatrist's choice depends on his experience and is somewhat trial and error. These antidepressants are habit-forming as they alter brain chemistry, basically serotonin levels. Nearly all antidepressants need four to eight weeks to build a threshold for optimum help. You can't take one only when you are having a bad day. Stopping a drug must be done with the help of a physician and is better accomplished gradually.

I cannot speak to the help of these drugs. In the 70's when I experienced depression there were no antidepressants. The drug I was on (possibly lithium) stopped my crying but paralyzed my emotions. I felt as though the world was going on around me. I couldn't laugh or cry nor could I feel anything. I had for all purposes joined the "walking dead."

Dialing up a depression hot line on the internet, I observed a discussion of patients on the side-effects of their antidepressants. Among the symptoms they experienced

---

[8]   Marianne Szegeby-Maszak, *"The career of a celebrity pill,"* U.S. News and World Report, August 6, 2001, p.38.

were apathy, lack of interest in sex, inability to urinate, dizziness, faintness, elevation in blood pressure.

In a world of technology new dangers for depression arise. Research conducted in 2014 by Dr. Brian Primack and colleagues from Univ. of Pittsburgh School of Medicine in 1787 adults 19-32 found that the more time young adults use social media (Facebook, Twitter, Snapchat, etc.) the higher their chances are of being depressed. On the average the study showed use of social media 61 minutes per day and visits to social media 30 times a week. (quoted by Marie Ellis from Journal of Depression and Anxiety.)

In a Sept. 21, 2010 article in the Washington Post, Donna St. George stated an NIH study of 7,000 students says that students targeted by cyber bullies "may be more likely to feel isolated, dehumanized or helpless at the time of attack. The most prevalent age was middle school, grades 6-8.

Dr. Bloomfield, a Yale trained psychiatrist, and associates appeared on a 1997 television program following the release of their book on the use of St. John's Wort. St. John's Wort (Hypericum) is the treatment of choice in England and Germany. Dr. Bloomfield interviewed two patients. One patient had been on six different antidepressants with no good results, many problems, and side effects. The other patient had been suicidal. Both said taking St. John's Wort caused a miracle in their lives and for the first time in many years, they felt excited and normal.

Dr. Norman Rosenthal M.D., chief of environmental psychiatry at the National Institute of Mental health in Bethesda, Maryland, recommended St. John's Wort especially for the elderly because it causes so few side effects and does not interact with other medications.

If you are looking for a psychiatrist or physician to help balance your chemicals, you might consider choosing one who will try natural and herbal therapy.

Below I am listing five products[9] which naturopaths recommend for depression. These products may be new and untried by your physician. Together you may be able to make a plan which will work for you.

5-hydroxytrytophan (5HTP) is the immediate precursor of serotonin. Tryptophan is the single amino acid from which serotonin is manufactured.

St. John's Wort Extract (0.3% Hypericin) Hypericin stops the activity of monoamine oxidase which is often elevated in depressed patients. (p.34)

L-Phenylalanine acts to suppress appetite and regulate a person's sense of well-being and maintains mood elevation. It is an amino acid out of which epinephrine and norepinephrine are made. (p.48)

Acetyl-L-Carnitine HCL used to stimulate cerebral blood flow as in Alzheimer's also elevates mood, and alleviates depression. (p.24)

SAM-e is a natural molecule produced primarily by the liver, It is an active form of the amino acid methionine found in most body tissues and fluids. SAM-e plays an important role in the building of neurotransmitters (brain chemicals) like serotonin, dopamine, norepinephrine, and epinephrine. It has been useful with arthritis and liver dysfunction.

---

[9]   Vitamin Research Products Catalogue, 1997-Carson City, NV, Phone 1-800-877-2447.

Vitamin Research Products and other pharmaceutical companies have nutrition experts in their research and development department who will answer questions for you and your doctor. The focus for medicine and for us should be prevention.

If antidepressants aren't working, look for other root causes for your depression. Do you need to live differently, or deal with difficult relationships?

In Chapter 11 "Laughter and Creativity," I discuss other ways to increase serotonin levels and ask the questions, what emotions and activities increase good brain chemicals and what ones are destructive? Are there other ways to increase serotonin levels than mood elevating drugs?

Make God, your Great Psychiatrist. Pray for direction and know that God often works hand in hand with doctors. There are times when we may find an antidepressant a bridge to wellness. Remember, God designed us in three parts i.e. spirit, mind and body. Don't let Him be your missing link. Treating only the mind-body leaves out the spirit. Putting God into the equation of doctors and drugs is crucial to our healing.

Unlike many in the medical community, I believe that depression can be a positive in our lives putting us into slow motion so that we can shift gears to a new life: wife to widow, married to divorced, active citizen to homebound caregiver. Depression slows us down, cuts out the extras, and pushes us toward simplicity and better priorities of life.

Although depression may be classified as a mental illness for some who are suicidal, violent or nonfunctional, for many of us it is part of the normal experience of life that occurs when we experience change or need a new path in life.

Through physical examinations, doctors can help us eliminate disease and poor nutrition as a cause of depression. They can ascertain whether prescribed medicines could be causing the side effects of depression. They can prescribe and monitor herbs or antidepressants to alter the chemicals of our brains. Medicine does have a role in depression and needs to be our ally in this great battle.

All the counseling and drug therapy available will do little good if disease is the basis of depression. It is incomprehensible that Humpty should live with depression for twenty years because of low thyroid, diabetes, low iron or other medical conditions.

One further area of physical health remains to explore-Nutrition.

Chapter 13

Can Medicine Help?

1. Do you have a doctor you can talk to?

2. When was your last good general physical? Have you ever been checked for low thyroid, mononucleosis, diabetes, or for the depression that is a side effect of some drugs?

3. Are you presently on antidepressant medication? Is it working? Should it be re-evaluated? Do you have any problems taking this medication?

4. Have you or could you discuss the use of the natural antidepressants with your prescribing physician i.e. the use of St. John's Wort, etc?

5. Are you being treated with a mind-body focus? Is it time to add God to the equation?

Prayer:
> *"Dear Lord, be my Great Psychiatrist.*
> *Guide me to any professional help you feel I need.*
> *Help me to use the best medicine as you direct.*
> *I ask this in Jesus name."*

Nutrition-The Missing Puzzle Piece?

"You are what you eat!"
(source unknown)

Waves of remembrance flooded my mind as I watched our daughter Julie alternately sitting and jumping up to gather forgotten food items, wipe spills, coax her two-year-old to eat a few bites of veggie, cut meat, spread butter, refill milk glasses. Dinner was exhausting, rather than sustaining. The meal over, she looked at the unappetizing mixture of cold remains. Fixing us a cup of hot tea, she kicked back and smiled. A typical dinner meal.

I smiled back remembering twenty years of serving meals. At that moment, we were soul mates. Could Julie's eating pattern put her at risk for depression? Does nutrition play an important role or any role in depression?

Nutrition may be one of the most overlooked contributors to depression. _All our brain chemicals are derived from the food we eat._

Let's begin with medicine's approach to depression and work backwards. If I am depressed, the psychiatrist may prescribe an antidepressant such as Prozac or Zoloft. The purpose of this drug is to raise my serotonin levels because medicine has learned that depressed people have lower serotonin, norepinephrine and dopamine levels.

What is serotonin? Serotonin is a neurotransmitter, an amine which is found in the blood and in the brain. Its job is to help the 10,000,000,000 brain cells communicate with each other to get the work of the body accomplished.

Serotonin, dopamine, norepinephrine, acetylcholine are all neurotransmitters.

Doctors try to increase serotonin by keeping enzymes from destroying serotonin thus increasing serotonin levels. Where does serotonin come from? These neurotransmitters are manufactured in the brain from substances called "precursors" in the presence of enzymes. The amino acid tryptophan-serotonin; amino acid tyrosine-norepinephrine; amino acid phenylanine=dopamine. **All three must be obtained through diet.**

Maureen Salaman author of *Foods That Heal*[10] tells us serotonin and dopamine are manufactured from foods such as poultry or fatlike substances called choline-wheat germ and egg yolk. In addition, Vit. B, C, iron and magnesium assist in the manufacture of neurotransmitters. Complicated? The only thing we need to remember is that *our brain chemicals are manufactured from the food we eat.* Food fuels our emotions and brain.

Elizabeth Somer, R.D. in her article, 'Food and Mood,' American Health April 1995 states, "Many people ignore profound effects food can have on mood, thought processes and energy level on a day to day basis. In fact, what we eat affects our memory, mood, vitality long before it affects our heart and bones. What we eat in the morning affects us in the afternoon. What we eat at night affects our sleep or sleeplessness."

She goes on to say that people experiencing negative moods, PMS, depression and food cravings often seek out chocolate and sweets. Chocolate stimulates the production

---

[10]   Maureen Salaman with James F. Scheer Foods That Heal MKS Inc. 1989 p. 205.

of serotonin. Certain foods such as sugar and caffeine and certain eating habits such as skipping meals may aggravate or even generate negative moods.[11]

But what do we eat? How do we nourish our body? And an even bigger question, like Julie, am I eating?

Let's look at some of the times in our lives when nutrient crises can be a problem.

Teen depression with the risk of suicide is high. Anorexia and bulimia are two teen eating disorders causing malnutrition, and poor health conditions. In both conditions, perfectionism and low self-esteem attached to physical appearance are root causes. Depression and distorted thinking are major components of both conditions.

A friend in her fifties recently coped with her only daughter's anorexia. The girl dropped to 62 pounds. Anne had been through several near death experiences with her daughter. This time, the daughter was running ten miles a day, working out at an exercise gym and waitressing. The people at the exercise gym recognized her poor health and weight loss and refused her entrance to their facility. The restaurant fired her afraid she was scaring the diners. The girl still saw herself as "fat" and refused to attend Thanksgiving or Christmas dinners with her family because of the food issue. A different kind of depression. Normal teens may suffer depression because of low self-esteem. As parents, we need to be alert to what's happening in our teen's lives.

Young single adults put in ten to fourteen-hour days sleeping in as late as possible, showering, skipping breakfast, too busy for lunch, returning home via the sub shop,

---

[11]   Elizabeth Somer, "Food and Mood," <u>American Health</u>, April 1995.

dropping exhausted on the couch to stare at Seinfeld reruns. Some become "grazers" dropping by the refrigerator (usually looking like Old Mother Hubbard's cupboard.) These same young adults may have well thought out exercise programs but fail to connect the truth that a body with no fuel will not perform well.

Women have additional nutrition problems:

Young working mothers stressed to the max are trying to live complicated lives as wife, mother and as a working woman. Hardly finding time to eat themselves, they are often responsible for their families' nutrition.

Women who deliver babies have hormonal and nutrient crises. Richard Kunin in his book, *Mega-Nutrition cites*[12] the fact that "psychiatric wards are filled with young mothers so depressed that many want to commit suicide. Creating a new life is a double nutrient burden. A nursing mother then has to produce a quart of milk daily to nurse the infant. Feeding the baby round the clock robs the mother of needed rest. To top it off, she then has the strain of adjusting to a different family relationship and lifestyle."

Midlife presents a new problem to women. Children grow up, and leave home. Our purpose in life removed, many of us have difficulty and find depression crouched and waiting to swallow us up. Our hormones are changing again (menopause) directly affecting our womanhood and beauty. Since hormones have a role in the conversion of foods to serotonin, we are again at risk both mentally and nutritionally.

---

[12] Caryl Stern, *Parade Magazine*, "Why Depression Is A Silent Killer, Sept. 1997.

And then lastly, are the seniors, those over 75 who are shrinking away. Spouses alone may find it too much trouble to cook for one. Poor appetite, and loss of hope can cause suicide to be a risk in older people. Death of a spouse, failing health, loss of hearing, not enough to do, and not wanting to be a burden to their children contribute to depression.

In each scenario through the lifespan nutrition is important. Women's nutrition is particularly affected by changes in the hormonal system during puberty, child bearing, and menopause.

What kind of nutrition do we need then? At present, a controversy about diet still battles. Should we eat carbohydrates or not? Fat or no fat? Is the food pyramid obsolete or appropriate? Do we need high protein or less protein as we get older?

Millions of words scream out some new dietary plan. Every issue of our ladies' magazines highlight some new research or discovery. We are bombarded with the *cabbage soup diet* (a diet for weight loss discovered for heart surgery patients), *the Atkins diet* (a high protein and fat diet which eliminates carbohydrates), *the diet based on blood types* which lists the foods which are medicinal for each blood type and the foods which are indigestible. (Type A – vegetarian or light poultry; Type O – beef eaters). *The Zone Diet* calls for a 40 carbohydrate, 30 protein, 30 fat combination instructing that if you get the proper proportions of the food groups you will be in the ideal zone for good health. And lastly, *Sugar Busters* a diet with say "no" to pasta, bread, cereal, rice, sugar-loaded foods. This diet suggests that sugar causes us to secrete insulin. Insulin causes our bodies to store excess fat.

Eat Right 4 Your Type	Dr. Peter S. D'Adamo Catherine Whitney	Claim eating the correct foods for your blood type essential for digestion. Based on twenty years of doctor's own research.
Mediterranean Diet Mayo Clinic Staff		Fruits, vegetables, whole grains, legumes & nuts, olive oil, red wine, limit red meat, eat fish & poultry, low fat dairy.
Sugar Busters	H. Leighton Steward Morrison C. Bethea Dr.'s: Sam S. Andrews Luis A. Balart	Diet steers you away from insulin-producing carbohydrates but not high-fiber ones.
The Zone	Barry Sears	"Protein adequate" diet gets you to "the zone." Hormonally speaking, by balancing levels of insulin and glucagons.

Since none of us have the same health needs, it would be presumptuous for me to recommend a particular diet for depression. I don't know if you are overweight, diabetic, have high cholesterol, low iron, or are one of those who need five small meals a day.

For most of us, following a balanced diet that contains all the basic food groups is important: breads, cereals, milk, cheese, butter, eggs, vegetables, poultry and meat, eight glasses of water a day or more. Use less caffeine, coffee, pops, sugar, and alcohol and food with additives. Use olive oil, or one of the new heart smart butters like Benecol. Make exceptions if you have a weight problem, are diabetic, allergic, or have high cholesterol.

We need to eat reasonable amounts of food, not starving or gorging ourselves, not loving ourselves with food because we are scared or lonely and keeping our diet as natural and chemical free as we can.

If we know we are battling depression, we must examine carefully what we are eating and be sure we have adequate nutrition. I can't say this enough.

All our good chemicals are formed from the food we eat. Vitamins are a concern at all periods of our life. Many vitamins and some minerals are involved in the production of serotonin.

Dr. Mark Gold in his book, *The Good News About Depression*[13] and Earl Mindell in *Shaping Up With Vitamins*[14] tell us that vitamins and minerals are involved in brain metabolism:

---

[13] Dr. Mark Gold, *The Good News About Depression*, Villard Books, New York 1984, pp. 121-132

[14] Earl Mindell, "Emotion Energizing" *Shaping Up With Vitamins*, Warner Books, 1985.

- Vit. B1--Above average amounts have been found to tranquilize anxious individuals and alleviate depression. (Oatmeal, whole wheat, peanuts, pork, and vegetables.)

- Vit, B6--Necessary for the function of the Adrenal Cortex and thus the proper production of natural antidepressants such as dopamine and norepinephrine.

  Not enough of this vitamin causes tingling in the limbs, numbness, and sensations of electric shocks.
      (Brewer's yeast, wheat bran, germ, cantaloupe, cabbage, molasses, milk, eggs, beef.)

- Pantothenic acid--A natural tension reliever when sufficient in diet. (Meat, whole grains, green leafy vegetables, nuts chicken, crude molasses.)

- Vit. B-12—Helps relieve irritability, improve concentration, increase energy, and maintain a healthy nervous system. It is found in meat and animal proteins and is lacking sometimes in vegetarians, and older people who do not eat enough meat. (Liver, beef, pork, eggs, milk and cheese.)

- Folic Acid—Essential for growth of all body cells. A deficiency has been found to be a contributing factor in mental illness. Low folic acid may cause burning feet, and restless leg syndrome. (Dark green leafy vegetables, carrots, egg yolk, cantaloupe, apricots, beans, and dark rye flour.)

- Vit. C—Essential for combating stress. Shortage of C produces tiredness, weakness, apathy, vague pains. A busy vitamin used to form connective tissue, and bones. It facilitates iron absorption and the action of folic acid and amino acids. (Citrus fruits, green leafy vegetables, tomatoes, cauliflower, berries, potatoes, sweet potatoes.)

Gold goes on to say that metals are also important in depression:

- Sodium (NA)—Controls water balance that seems to be a concern in PMS mood disturbance. (Salt, shellfish, carrots, beets, artichokes, dried beef, bacon.)

- Potassium (K)—Depression is the main mental manifestation of a potassium deficiency. (Citrus fruits, watercress, green leafy vegetables, mint leaves, sunflower seeds, bananas and potatoes.)

- Iron—One study showed that half of all pre-menopausal women and a third of all children do not receive enough iron, a mineral associated with low energy and depression. (Raw clams, dried peaches, red meat, egg yolk, oysters, nuts, beans, asparagus, molasses, and oatmeal.)

- Calcium—Alleviates tension, irritability, and promotes relaxation. In too large a quantity or too little will definitely cause depression. (Milk, cheese, soybeans, salmon, peanuts, walnuts, dried beans, green vegetables.)

- Magnesium—Known as the anti-stress mineral. Lack shows up in agitation, disorientation, confusion, anxiety, and even hallucinations. A deficit produces symptoms of depression. (Figs, lemons, grapefruit, yellow corn, nuts, almonds, seeds and apples.)

- Zinc—Promotes mental alertness and aids in proper brain function. More than fifty enzymes need zinc in order to function properly. Loss of appetite, taste, and smell, immune system functioning, mental slowing, irritability, emotional disorders and rough skin are related to zinc. Zinc deficiency depression is seen particularly among the elderly. (Round steak, lamb chops, pork loin, wheat germ, pumpkin seeds, eggs, ground mustard.)

The importance of nutrition cannot be overemphasized in relation to depression. Maureen Salaman author of *Foods That Heal*[15] tells us: "Once the late Dr. Carlton Fredericks gave me his candid opinion on mood elevating drugs as opposed to vitamins and minerals in coping with emotional disorders such as depression. Drugs hide the symptoms and nutrients remove the cause."

Check your actual eating pattern by writing down everything you eat in a few days. If you see a problem, correct it or ask a nutrition expert to counsel you.

In the next chapter, we will examine other ways to boost serotonin and endorphin levels. Take away these truths:

---

[15] Maureen Salaman with James F. Scheer *Foods That Heal* MKS Inc. 1989 p.205

1. All our brain chemicals are derived from the food we eat.

2. All three brain neurotransmitters (serotonin, norepinephrine, and dopamine) must be obtained through diet

We are what we eat!

Chapter 14

Nutrition-The Missing Puzzle Piece?

Exercises:

1. Analyze your nutrition. Write down everything you eat including snacks for one week. Be honest. Also write down the time of day you are eating. How does it compare with the suggested nutrition?

2. What vitamins and minerals are you taking? Visit a vitamin store or have a nutritionist, vitamin expert, or physician help you choose wise ones for your time of life.

3. Do you overeat or barely get enough nutrition? If you are starving for chocolate or carbohydrates your body may be signaling low serotonin levels. Try to eat a balanced diet. Don't let emotions rob your mental and physical health.

4. Keep in mind that the body is the house of your Spirit. What changes could you make to take better care of yourself?

Laughter and Creativity

"Laff everytime you pheel tickled. And
laff once in awhile, enyhow."
Josh Billings

One summer afternoon, the girls and I floated lazily on air mattresses. The sapphire lake mirrored fluffy white clouds.

"Laugh, Mom."

I opened one eye squinting at the offending daughter. These girls were always putting me on. "No one's told a joke. What do you want me to laugh at?"

"C'mon, Mom. I can't remember the last time you laughed."

Neither could I. It had been years. I made an effort to laugh. It was so phony and artificial that hearing it, I began to smile.

"That's no laugh!" the girls countered.

"Try laughing like Santa Claus."

I let out a "ho, ho, ho, then a hee, hee, hee." A torrent of tear-jerking laughter spilled out of me like a rushing waterfall. I couldn't stop. I was gasping. Laughing refreshed me and I felt purified. Worn out from the exercise, I floated content and peaceful. The cork was out of the bottle. My sense of humor returned. From then on, even little things triggered a fresh burst of laughter.

Norman Cousins, who suffered from a chronic fatal condition, wrote about his personal experience in combating pain in his book, *Anatomy of An Illness*.[16] With the cooperation of his friend and physician, Norman moved into a private suite where he began to watch funny movies—Candid Camera episodes and his favorite Marx Brothers movies—laughter therapy. He found ten minutes of laughter had an anesthetic effect and would give him two hours of pain free sleep. (By the way, Norman's disease went into remission). Doctors now believe that laughter increases endorphins which produce a morphine like peacefulness in the body. Researchers tell us that T cell and B cells are affected strengthening the immune system as well.[17]

Science News ran an article, "Depressed To The Bone." The article stated research proved reoccurring bouts of depression actually caused loss of bone density. The outcome-osteoporosis.[18]

Through laughter, we release good chemicals increasing our endorphins (peptides released in the brain that have a pain relieving effect like morphine) and serotonin levels. Serotonin, a complex amine found in blood and the brain, helps transmit chemical and electrical signals through the body as a neurotransmitter.

With the discovery that serotonin is low in depression a new frontier of possibilities opens. Can I change the chemical levels in my brain? Let's look at some activities I believe change and affect our brain's chemical climate: exercise, housework, creative endeavors, listening to music,

---

[16]   Norman Cousins, *Anatomy of an Illness*, Aug. 1991, *Bantam Doubleday Publishers*

[17]   Family Circle, "Are Giggles Good for You?" August 1999.

[18]   Science News, Vol. 146, *"Depressed to the Bone"*, Nov. 26, 1994.

singing or playing an instrument, meditation, writing, and pets.

Professional athletes and runners experience "highs." In fact, runners tell me sometimes they run to have this euphoria. Running causes the heart to pump harder forcing more oxygen into the blood stream which supplies the brain. Chemicals are changed; endorphins are released from the exercise. According to a newspaper article run by the Tribune Media Services entitled "The Challenge: How to use exercise to alleviate depression," exercise professional Judi Sheppard Missett stated that 'new research indicates that exercise may be as helpful as drugs in reducing or eliminating symptoms in clinically depressed individuals.'

Looking back on my life, I thought just getting through the day was goal enough. Tell me to exercise and I would have smiled thinking you really didn't get it. I hardly had enough energy to tie my tennis shoes much less waste it on exercise. Wouldn't exercise use up the small amount of energy I had? Exercise of any kind was the last thing I wanted to do.

In depression, our system slows down, however, low energy levels and a desire to sleep vanish if we force ourselves to exercise. *Exercise stimulates good chemicals in my blood stream and brain.* Push yourself. *Begin to put regular exercise, three times a week into your schedule.* Begin with walking but running, hiking, working out in a gym, water aerobics, biking, rollerblading are all excellent exercise. Find a sport you enjoy.

Consider joining an exercise class. Attending a class will help you begin a new discipline. Or consider playing volleyball, basketball, softball with a community or church league.

An interesting aside, the nutrition book by Dr. Peter S. D'Adamo with Catherine Whitney Eat Right 4 Your Type based on blood types lists exercises for various blood types. According to this theory, people with blood type A need slower paced activities such as golf, walking or mild water aerobics. Type O's, on the other hand, need fast paced exercise-jogging, racket ball, tennis, basketball, soccer.[19] Dancing is also good exercise. If you have no partner, try line dancing. Classes are offered at all age levels from senior citizen to teens and tots.

Exercise increases good mood lifting chemicals.

A few years ago, I began taking classes in watercolor painting. Concentrating on the orchestration of the painting, a strange thing happened. I became oblivious to time, phones, voices, etc. A different part of my brain took charge. During this period, no worries, anxious thoughts, or problems entered my mind. I felt peaceful and calm at the end of a painting session.

In her book *Drawing on the Artist Within* author Betty Edwards speaks of using drawing to kick start right brain activity.[20] The right brain is the emotional side of the brain, the creative side. The left brain is the linguistic, mathematical and logical side.

Finding activities which stimulate right brain activity assist us in our control of depression. Activities which

---

[19]   Dr. Peter S. D'Adamo with Catherine Whitney, *Eat Right 4 Your Type*, G.P. Putnam's Sons, NY 1996.

[20]   Betty Edwards, *Drawing on the Artist Within*, Simon and Shuster, 1986.

produce pleasure and peacefulness alter chemical levels and increase serotonin.

In Genesis, we read "God created…. And it was good." It excited God to create. Creating also seems to release a good chemical response in our bodies. Taking yam and knitting a sweater, planting and nurturing a vegetable or a flower garden, turning a piece of wood into a birdhouse or a chair, sewing pieces of cloth into a quilt, shaping clay into a pot, release good creative energy-thus, good chemicals. You are stimulating the right brain. *Creating* seems to release a good chemical response in our bodies.

Music soothes the soul, relaxes tires bodies and minds and acts as a sedative. David played on the lyre for King Saul to calm his tortured mental state. Singing or playing musical instruments thrusts us into a different area of the brain again creating a new chemicals. (Also, it is one of the few activities we can carry from earth to heaven—the angels sing!)

One summer, I began to think about singing in our church choir. Christian music always stirred me deeply. I ran into a church acquaintance in Target. "What are you going to participate in this year?" she asked.

I wasn't sure at that point, but mentioned the idea of singing in the choir. Holding me back was the fear that I hadn't sung in a choir since eighth grade, could only read music from middle C one octave each way, and could never get on key to sing Happy Birthday.

She smiled and said, "You know, my husband sings in the choir. What do you think you sing?"

This was the 64-dollar-question. Visions of standing in front of 40 people to discover whether I was an alto or soprano terrified me. "I don't know, I like to sing the melody," I told her. "Well, tell them you are a soprano. At choir practice try to stand next to a strong soprano."

I thanked her and decided to try this strange unexplored territory. Looking back, I'm sure the Lord was drawing me into that choir. Since then, I have sung in four church choirs. All were glad to have an additional body to sing. Singing not only is strenuous lung exercise putting more oxygen into my blood but makes me feel exhilarated and changes my mood. Between the beautiful words and the lovely melodies, I fill up my emotional gas tank.

We can join a choir, a community chorale, sing in our car to the radio or CD player, or just sing in the shower. From crickets to coyotes, nature was created with a song to sing. Sing your song, make your joyful, or soulful noise.

Pediatric authorities tells us to play beautiful music for the unborn fetus (Mozart.) Someone sees the connection.

If music hasn't been part of your life, consider it as something new to experience. Take a risk. Be willing to begin, to be the only one on a note.

Music soothes us and fills up our reservoir!

Stress, on the other hand, causes bad chemicals to flow and provides a negative atmosphere for disease to flourish. Long-term stress alters our immune system leaving us prey to chronic disease like fibromyalgia, and chronic fatigue syndrome. Likewise, anxiety, fear, and anger stimulate bad chemicals and enzymes in our system. These emotions are forerunners to heart attack, colon problems and even cancer. Do they cause a heightened production of enzymes—cortisol, acids, which destroy serotonin, norepinephrine and dopamine? Does their constant presence in our system trigger immune failure as our bodies begin to consider our own cells the enemy and produce allergic reactions to… We can be very suspicious, can't we?

Writing out your feelings and frustrations is therapeutic. Sitting down after a loved one dies and writing a letter telling them how we feel can help us to work through the grief process. Writing feelings of anger or upset releases the pent-up volcanic passion of destructive emotions.

A few years ago I wrote my husband a letter about what he meant to me and how I viewed retirement as a "beginning," not an ending. I laid out my goals 1. to breathe new life into our relationship 2. to find and act on God's purpose for my remaining years through writing and women's retreats 3. to become a watercolor artist, and 4. to make some new friends.

The letter helped him understand where I was. It cleared the air. He needed to know I wasn't discontent with our life but just had some discoveries to make.

I spent almost three years writing adventures that showed the love and care of God in a 25-year-period for our family. I self-published *Along The Way* and gave it to my children, a few friends and family. All the hours I focused on writing of God's love and care strengthened my belief that *He is* and *He does care*. You, too, can write a family book to show God's love in your family. You will be focusing on the good rather than the negative when you undertake this project.

One of the main tenants of the *Artist's Way* is to do three pages of writing each day to empty out our feelings and clear our channels.

Writing is an outlet for emotions.

I mentioned earlier that psychiatric professionals are beginning to advocate meditation. (See chapter 9) There are many kinds of meditation: deep breathing, emptying the mind, visualization, and of course, transcendental meditation which includes repeating a calming word over and over (mantra).

In studying the Bible I have found three forms of meditation:

1. Psalm 46 states, "Be still and know that I am God." We can be quiet before the Lord and listen for His still small voice.

2. Meditating on the scriptures *fills the mind* rather than emptying it. In Joshua, Ch. 1, vs. 8, we are told, "you shall meditate on (scripture) day and night, that you may observe and do according to all that is written in it; for then you shall make your way prosperous, and you shall deal wisely and have good success.

3. The third type of meditation is prayer. The psalms contain many examples of prayer as do St. Paul's writing.

Meditation quiets the soul and puts us in touch with God.

A chronically depressed friend unable to reach out to people purchased a small friendly dog. She fed, walked, played games and sat holding the little fellow on her lap. Her eyes sparkled when she spoke of Mac's antics. He loved her unconditionally, got so excited when she came home he nearly wagged his tail off, jumping into the air and barking. Mac made a difference. Pets need us, accept us, love us, and are faithful and loyal to us. They bolster our sagging self-esteem—all for a little love and a dog cookie. Pets calm us and relieve our loneliness.

Pets are also therapeutic and change our chemicals.

In the olden days, I remember my Grandma, the mother of ten children and thousands of grandchildren, using her housework to stay happy. Grandma boiled her dishwater on top of the stove to wash her dishes. While the water was boiling, she walked over to a small table in her kitchen which held a jigsaw puzzle.

Grandma canned millions of cans of cherries, tomatoes, beans, peaches, in the summer for eating in the winter. She always had something tasty to give as a gift from her garden. Washing windows and mopping floors weren't done by a cleaning service.

The only one depressed in Grandma's house was Grandpa. Grandma was too busy taking care of him and the family. (Just joking.) But diving into a physical work project will also make the good chemicals flow. Dressing up a room with a new coat of paint, or giving the bathroom the once over with heavenly pine smelling cleaners are an antidote for the blahs.

Be creative in changing your own chemical balance. Antidepressants are not the only choice you have. When black moods try to overpower you, dig a garden, take the dog for a walk, write a letter, or wash a window!

Chapter 15

Laughter and Creativity
(are good medicine!)

Exercises:

1. When is the last time you laughed out loud? Laughter experiment: Try to laugh out loud. (Go in to the shower, a closet, *mimic* Santa, but really have a hearty laugh.) How do you feel?

2. What creative activities could you add to your life? A course? Sewing lessons? Art lessons? Choose at least one new activity and begin.

3. Think about this: There were no cars in Bible times. People walked miles to visit one another. Moses walked the desert for forty years. Paul walked all over Europe. Ask yourself, 'Is my life too sedentary?' Count the hours you sit at a desk or in a lounge chair. Do something to make your blood circulate.

4. Make a regular exercise plan three times a week. Start with 30-45 minute walks three times a week or if you're brave, every day. Add another activity: biking, tennis, golf, running and aerobics.

VI. The Winner... Humpty!

Chapter 16. "Singin' In The Rain"

"Singin' In The Rain"[21]

"Im singin' in the rain,
Just singin' in the rain
What a glorious feeling,
I'm happy again!

When most of us run for cover, duck under an umbrella or stay inside avoiding the rain altogether, Gene Kelly is singing. Not only is he singing in the rain but he is dancing, smiling, exuding energy and joy!

The question for many of us when we encounter the rain in our lives (into each life a little rain must fall) is 'How Then Shall I Live?'

- When my life is so difficult that I don't even want to get up in the morning.
- When I've given up my job to take care of an Alzheimer parent, husband or wife, sweetheart.
- When my son on drugs is put in prison for holding a gun while his friends rob a drugstore.
- When my eighteen-year-old falls off a scaffold while washing windows on a skyscraper and dies.
- When I am diagnosed with cancer and face months of chemotherapy and radiation as well as the question, 'will I live?'

---

21 "Singin' In The Rain", music written by Herb Ncio Brown, and Arthur Freed. The Hollywood Revue-1929 then MGM musical Singin' In The Rain-1952.

- When I face daily responsibility of raising children as a single parent with little income, scared, tired.
- When I lose my mate, my friend, my love.

How then shall I live? Why, if God loves me, does He allow me to suffer like this? Why doesn't He protect me from harm?

If you are in depression because of the difficult life you live and have given up or burned out, you can have an alternative. Instead of thinking, "Why, me?" You can say, "Why not me?"

A couple of years ago, my brother Mike fell and broke his collarbone. X-rays showed a large tumor in his shoulder muscle. The doctors advised him not to worry stating this kind of tumor was rarely malignant. Against medical advice, Mike insisted on surgery. The surgeon removed much of the tumor but because of the crippling effect it would have on Mike's life, he didn't remove it all. Tissue study revealed a malignant lymphoma. Mike made a wise decision. Chemotherapy and radiation followed. What was Mike's attitude? He said, "Sis, cancer happens to anyone. Why shouldn't it happen to me?"

The long battle of chemotherapy and radiation began. He wore baseball caps when his hair fell out. (This made us all smile as he was really quite sophisticated and baseball caps seemed out of character.) He embraced the days he felt energetic, and rested the days the chemo or radiation made him feel like he had been run over by a truck. He accepted the battle, reached out to God for strength and became a light of hope for all of us who knew what was going on in his life. He was "singin' in the rain."

When we come to that point in our life, the point when we no longer have the strength to continue, perhaps it is time to ask the Great Physician for his help, *"Lord, show me how to live my life in joy not just to get through each day. Show me how to live victoriously. Show me how to sing in the rain."*

Living in joy when circumstances are intolerable causes an unearthly light to shine. This light radiating from your life, becomes hope for others who see you and say, "How can she live so happily with such a difficult life?" If they ask you, you will have an opportunity to tell them about your Great Physician.

Each winter, February was my most difficult month. Spring was still months ahead. The joy and excitement of Christmas was over and I always experienced a real let down as did my husband's widowed mother. George called my brother who was a foreign service officer stationed in the Bahamas. Would he like a couple of guests for a week? My brother opened his home to us. He welcomed us and made every effort to show us a good time.

While we were visiting, a friend of his invited us to her parents' home for a formal dinner. I was seated next to an English woman. She drew me into a private conversation. "You look so peaceful. I thought someone said you had six children at home?"

I smiled, "I do."

"I've only seen that kind of peace from one other woman," she continued.

"And who was that?" I asked.

"A woman evangelist came to the Bahamas for a tent crusade. I invited my friends; I thought they would get a kick out of it."

"What was your reaction?"

"My friends were bored, but I could feel her peace. She said it came from Jesus. She spoke of Jesus this and Jesus that."

I was shocked. The woman was surprised to feel peace coming from me. With six children and a busy life she expected to sense worry and hurry.

"I also have experienced Jesus." I said quietly. "You can, too; all you have to do is ask Him to come into your life and your heart."

In difficult circumstances, can we learn to live so that others will notice there is something different, something special? Is it possible that having peace and joy in difficult scenarios of your life can attract people?

Robert Schuler tells this story in his book, *The Be-Happy Attitudes.*[22]
(paraphrase) Dr. Schuller had seen many kinds of boat wakes from cruise ships to tiny row boats but as he was flying over the ocean, he noticed a mammoth trail which appeared to be a wake. He wondered what kind of craft could cause such a large wake? Soon the plane was in position for him to see the vessel causing the wake. He spotted a tiny object and realized he was looking at the telescope of a submarine. Gradually, the submarine surfaced. A small craft, how could it make such a gigantic wake? Then revelation hit. The wake was created because the sub had been in deep waters and come to the surface.'

Our deep waters (trials) can make a wake for the world around us to observe. Are you making the most of the wake you are creating?

---

[22]   Robert Schuller, "I Can Choose To Be Happy Anyway" p.210, *The Be-Happy Attitudes*, Word Publishing, 1985.

When Christine Meyer Clifford of Denver was diagnosed with breast cancer, laughter was the last thing on her mind. After surgery, she decided to focus on laughter. Once she had found laughter, she realized it was all around her. The more she laughed, the stronger she grew. The night before chemotherapy began, her friends threw her a "chemotherapy shower." Sixteen women were invited and asked to bring a hat. When she entered the room she could feel the tension. To break the ice one friend asked, "Christine would you like a cigarette?" "No thanks," she replied, "I already have cancer." Christine wrote a book of her experiences with cancer and called it, "Not Now... I'm Having a No Hair Day!" Christine was making a wake.[23]

St. Paul was imprisoned several times. On one occasion after being beaten he and his companion were placed in the inner dungeon in the stocks. Hands and feet shackled in the dark, damp, rat-infested dungeon, what did they do? Of course, they prayed and sang hymns. (Acts 16:25) They were *singin' in the rain*. The startled jailer had probably never heard anyone sing in the inner dungeon. Then there was an earthquake. The jailer, afraid the prisoners would escape, drew his sword and was about to kill himself.

Paul caught his attention and began to talk to him. He told the jailer about Jesus—the good news that God had sent His son to save his soul. The jailer and his family were converted to faith in God. Why? Did the singing in the dungeon cause a wake that the jailer was watching?

Paul tells us that he knew how to be content in whatever circumstances he found himself: stoned and left for dead,

---

23   Christine Meyer Clifford, "Hope, Laughter, Positive Thinking," The Anchora Magazine—Delta Gamma, Fall 1998.

shipwrecked, bitten by a viper, beaten, imprisoned, hungry, or cold. He also found himself surrounded by friends and loved ones, a special guest, entertained by kings. He was content. Whatever God allowed in his life, he knew nothing would be wasted.

I think, it would be safe to say that many of us with depression have not grasped the contentment philosophy.

In Romans Ch. 5:3, Paul tells us *"but we rejoice in our sufferings, because we know that suffering produces perseverance; perseverance, character and character, hope."* Our sufferings have purpose. God can take anything in our lives and turn it to blessing.

I challenge you to live your life in joy not just barely making it from one day to the next. God is faithful. He is our Great Psychiatrist and will walk along with us whether we are shifting gears from one life to another or beginning a whole new life.

"Singin' in The Rain"

Picture Humpty, a little cracked but back on the wall, a smile on his face. Listen, do you hear it?

> "I'm singin' in the rain,
> Just singin' in the rain,
> What a glorious feelin'
> I'm happy again."

Way to go, Humpty!

Chapter 16

Singing In The Rain

1. Can you think of other examples of people who have a difficult life and still cope well?

2. Give an example of someone who took a terrible loss and made something good come out of it.

3. What kind of wake are you making? Can you accept your present reality and begin to be thankful for your life?

4. Read the Book of Esther in the Bible. A Jewish captive in a Persian land, Esther becomes a wife of King Xerxes. How does Esther cope? How does God make something good come out of her captivity?

5. What does God do after all Job's suffering? (Job 42:1 0-17). Is it possible for God to bless and restore us?

Bibliography- Christian

Ch. 1   Florence Littauer, *Your Personality Tree*, Word Publishing, July 1989 (Book and video series)

Ch. 4   Dr. Charles Allen, *God's Psychiatry*, Fleming H. Revel Co. 1953, p. 1.

Ch. 5   Hannah Whitall Smith, *The God who is Enough*, Moody Press, Chicago, 1956.

Ch. 7   Beth Moore, *Praying God's Word*, Ch. 12 "Overcoming Depression," p. 249.

Ch. 8   Cecil Murphey, *Invading the Privacy of God*, Servant Publications, Ann Arbor, MI. 1997 Becky Tirabassi, *My Partner Prayer Notebook* author of *Let Prayer Change Your Life*, Thomas Nelson Publishers, 1984, 86, 90.

Ch. 11   John Powell, SJ. *Happiness is An Inside Job*, *"Do I Accept Myself?"* Tabor Publishing, Allen Texas, 1989

Ch. 12   Florence Littauer, *Silver Boxes,* "Boxes of Broken Dreams," Word Publishing, May 1990, Pages, 124,125.

Ch. 16   Robert Schuller, *The Be-Happy Attitudes*, "I Can Choose To Be Happy Anyway," Word Books, Waco Texas, 1985, p. 210.

Bibliography-Medicine

Dr. Harold Bloomfield, M.D. and Peter McWilliams, *"New Hope New Help for Depression," Good Housekeeping* v. 219, p. 58, Aug. 94. The doctors give an excellent description of a good physical examination. What needs to be checked for depression in terms of disease, nutrition, blood tests?

Dr. Harold Bloomfield, M.D. Peter McWilliams *How to Heal Depression Prelude* press, May, 1994. A simple book which can be given to the depressed with short ar spans.

Peter McWilliams, Mikael Nordfors, Harold H Bloomfield *Hypericum (St. John's Wort) and Depression*, Prelude Press, June 1997. Two noted psychiatrists report on research of St. John's Wort on the chronically depressed.

Richard Brown, Carol Colman, Teodoro Bottiglieri, *Stop Depression Now: SAM-e the Breakthrough Supplement that works as well As Prescription Drugs in Half the Time with No Side Effects.* Putnam Publishing Group, July 1999. Richard Brown a practicing psycho-pharmacologist and associate professor of clinical psychiatry at Columbia University has used the supplement SAM-e for five years. Teodoro Bottiglieri-PhD is the world's leading expert on SAM-e and its effect on depression and arthritis. A good book to give your doctor: 1. self-assessment 2. Information on how to use SAM-e 3. Diet plan emphasizes food and vitamins which will make you feel better and worse. 4. Lifestyle changes and therapeutic techniques to help.

Les Carter Ph.D and Frank Minirth M.D. *The Freedom from Depression Workbook* Thomas Nelson Publishers Nashville, 1995. 12 part plan. Helps you know if you are depressed. Ch. 7 tells ways to find release from control of strong, imperative people who have a mold for you to fit, high expectations and fluctuating moods. Case studies from work with the depressed at the Minirth Clinics.

Colette Dowling *You Mean I Don't Have To Feel This Way?* Scribner 1991, and Bantam Books, 1993 NY. This is an excellent book for helping you understand serotonin, neurotransmitters, cells, as it applies to antidepressants and depression, anxiety, phobias, obsessions.

Gary Emery, Ph.D, and James Campbell, M.D. *Rapid Relief for Emotional Distress.* 1986. Rawson Associates: New York. Ch. 1 pp. 5-10. Explains the theory of Choice vs. Blame. Helps one look at the choices that each difficult situation presents. Calls for a vision of how you want to be. Purports view you own your own point of view, feelings, and have "response ability" only for yourself. Cannot make choices for someone else. Breaks down some distorted thinking of depressed people.

Daniel Goleman Ph.D. *Emotional Intelligence*, Ch. 11 Mind and Medicine, Bantam Books, Oct. 1995 N.Y., N.Y. This chapter shows research that finds a connection between the neuro system and the immune system affected by stress, hormones, anxiety.

Lester Grinspoon, M.D. and James B. Bakalar, J.D. *Depression and Other Mood Disorders,* The Harvard Medical School Mental Health Review, President and Fellows of Harvard College, 1995. Pp. s 10,1l.

Carol Hart, *Secrets of Serotonin* St. Martin's Mass Market Paper, Sept. 1996 reveals changes in diet and lifestyle which can elevate serotonin levels.

Christ Zois, M.D. with Patricia Fogarty *Think Like a Shrink,* The Stonesong Press, Inc. Warner Books, NY, NY 1992. Explains psychotherapy which is short term and confronts the problems directly not allowing the patient denial or avoidance. A form of psychotherapy.

Bibliography-Nutrition

Dr. Peter S. D'Adamo with Catherine Whitney, *4 Blood Types, 4 Diets Eat Right 4 Your Type,* G.P. Putnam's Sons, NY 1996. Based on doctors personal research this book claims each blood type has foods which are medicinal and foods that are problems.

Richard Kunin, *Mega-Nutrition*, NY: McGraw-Hill Co. 1980 p. 150

Earl Mindell's *Shaping Up With Vitamins* Warner Books, 1985.

Julia Ross, *The Diet Cure: The 8-Step Program to Rebalance your Body Chemistry and End Food Craving, Weight Problems and Mood Swings-NOW.* Viking Press, May 1999. Judith Ross is a nutritional psychologist. The gist of the Diet Care Plan is that food allergies, hormonal irregularities, blood sugar swings and thyroid dysfunction... cause biochemical imbalances that lead to food addiction and weight gain. These symptoms can usually be eradicated or helped by proper diet and supplements.

Maureen Salaman with James F. Scheer, *Foods That Heal* MKS Inc. 1989, p.205. Contains a section on depression. Includes a discussion of foods that heal and hurt; vitamins, minerals, herbs; recipes, doctor's opinions and research.

Maureen Kennedy Salaman, John P. Trowbridge *All Your Health Questions Answered Naturally*, Bay to Bay Distribution July 1998.

Dr. Barry Sears and Bill Lauren Harper Collins, June 1995 *The Zone: A Dietary Road Map To Lose Weight Permanently: Reset Your Genetic Code; Prevent Disease: Achieve Maximum Physical Performance* The Zone is "that mysterious but very real state in which your body and mind work together at their ultimate best." Based on Nobel Prize-winning research, the premise is simple: Calorie counting doesn't work. Maintaining the correct ratio of fats, proteins and carbohydrates is what is important. Stresses eating a balanced diet with 40% Carbohydrates, 30% protein, 30% fat. Author claims the Zone is a lifestyle not a diet.

Elizabeth Somer, *Food and Mood: The Complete Guide to Eating Well and Feeling Your Best.* 2nd. Edition 1999. Good Morning America nutrition correspondent. Stresses connection between what we eat and our emotional health.

Elizabeth Somer, *Nutrition for Women: The Complete Guide.* Henry Holt Publishing, Jan. 1995. A practical, handy book on women's nutrition. Current scientific data from more than 2,000 recent studies. Covers fertility, fatigue, PMS, osteoporosis, pregnancy, menopause.

H. Leighton Steward, *Sugar Busters: Cut Sugar To Trim Fat*, Ballantine Books *May 1998* Say "No" to pasta, bread, cereal, rice, sugar loaded foods. Sugar causes us to secrete insulin. Insulin causes our bodies to store excess fat.

Vitamin Research Products Catalogue, Carson City, NV, Phone 1-800-877-2447 (Herbal medicines which can be used in depression i.e. St. John's Wort et al.

Judith Wills, *The Food Bible*, Fireside Books--a division of Simon and Schuster, Inc. April 1999. Food is not only vital fuel but also vital medicine. Sec. I How to get a balanced diet. Discussion of carbohydrates, fats, proteins. Sec. 2 Food as medicine-specific ailments paired with helpful foods, herbs, vitamins, and foods to avoid. Sec. 3 What foods to eat at different stages of your life. Sec. 4 A 4 wk. weight control plan. Sec. 5 Recipes with nutrition breakdown. Sec. 6 Nutritional components of 400 foods.

Putting Humpty Dumpty Together Again

Metamorphosis

I'm standing on the shore of the lake.
Angry purple and black clouds rush
past the devastation below.

A hundred year old elm lies on its side
Roots exposed to wind and rain.
Boats float upside down in the gray water.
Power lines, broken, spit electricity--
communication disrupted.

Then

The sun breaks through the clouds
Shooting rays of hope and light.
A rainbow...gossamer...iridescent forms
a bridge between the storm past and the golden sunshine.

A picture of my life...
The rainbow promises a new life
And I, Humpty, stand in the sunshine.

Sylvia Burke

About the Author

Sylvia Burke graduated with a B.S. in Nursing from Indiana University. She writes as a nurse, a person who has experienced depression, and a Bible teacher. Her nursing experience in obstetrics and hospice give her a unique perspective to combine with her love of the Bible and belief that its counsel is alive today.

She states 2 Corin:1:3, 4 tells us "to comfort those who like us are hurting with the comfort we have received of God." Therein lies the purpose of Humpty. Her faith in God as the Great Psychiatrist offers an unusual approach to depression--Spirit, Mind, and Body.

Sylvia and her husband George (55 years) are retired in the Phoenix area and enjoy travel adventures. They are parents of six, grand- parents of eleven.

Her hobbies include singing in a choir, teaching Bible studies for women, and taking pictures of sunsets and nature which she translates into watercolors and quilts. She is also the author of a fiction trilogy entitled 2025 The Guardian, 2025 City of Gold, and 2025 The Remnant.

Printed in the United States
By Bookmasters